The Future

C000133465

www.bookcrossing.com
BCID 264-16375243
Visit the website and make a journal
entry

The Future of Community

Reports of a Death
Greatly Exaggerated

Edited by
Dave Clements, Alastair Donald,
Martin Earnshaw and Austin Williams

PLUTO PRESS
www.plutobooks.com

First published 2008 by Pluto Press
345 Archway Road, London N6 5AA

www.plutobooks.com

British Library Cataloguing in Publication Data
A catalogue record for this book is available from the British Library

ISBN   978 0 7453 2817 1   Hardback
ISBN   978 0 7453 2816 4   Paperback

Library of Congress Cataloging in Publication Data applied for

10   9   8   7   6   5   4   3   2   1

Designed and produced for Pluto Press by
Chase Publishing Services Ltd, Fortescue, Sidmouth, EX10 9QG, England
Typeset by Stanford DTP Services, Northampton, England
Printed and bound in the European Union by
CPI Antony Rowe, Chippenham and Eastbourne

NOTE: WRITTEN IN 2007 BEFORE THE TORY GOVERNMENTS, PUBLIC SPENDING CUTS AND THE PANDEMIC. THIS IS NOW **Contents** LESS OF A POLICY ISSUE THAN IT USED TO BE. ALSO WRITTEN BEFORE BREXIT, WHICH HAS PUT A WHOLE NEW COMPLEXION ON POLITICAL LIFE,

Acknowledgements

This book has its origins in the Future of Community Festival organised by the Future Cities Project and these essays have been developed from that early work. Our thanks go to the individual authors of these essays and to the speakers, contributors and participants at the Future of Community Festival with special thanks to Tricia Austin, Peter Cleak and Despina Hadjilouca of Central St Martins and Deirdre Malynn of the Cochrane Theatre without whose help the debate would never have taken place. Thanks to Frank Furedi, James Panton and Alan Hudson for their critical comments during the book's early stages. We are indebted to Patrick Hayes, Richard Reynolds, Stephen Rowland, Michael Owens, Mark Charmer, Pete Smith, Astrid Kirchner, Shirley Lawes, Justine Brian, Rob Lyons, Jenny Davey, Joe Kaplinsky, Kumiko Shimizu and Maisie Rowe who in various ways made this project possible. Finally, we thank our publishers at Pluto Press.

Introduction:
Who Needs Community Anyway?

Austin Williams

Nowadays, politicians and pundits alike accept that societal ties have loosened and that consequently there is less cohesion in society. Since Putnam started the ball rolling, many commentators have accepted that there is a widespread 'sense of civic malaise' (Putnam 2001) arising from the unravelling of local social bonds and have highlighted the dangers that such societal fragmentation implies. While police chiefs suggest that 'communities are under siege from a hardcore of antisocial, under-age drinkers' (Bannerman and Ford 2007) the decline of community can be blamed on everything from the arrival of Starbucks (*Daily Mail* 2006) and Tesco (Winterson 2007) to the use of the motor car (Lunts 2003) or the aeroplane (Russell 2008).

Whatever one's particular choice of causes for community's decline, since the turn of the new millennium there has been a growing recognition in political and academic circles that there is a fracturing of trust and cooperation in people's everyday interactions with each other. However, nowadays, not only are we concerned about the erosion of communities but we are prone to paranoia about complete societal collapse

[handwritten: HAS THAT CHANGED, SINCE THE PANDEMIC 2020?]

(Diamond 2005), or even about the end of civilisation as we know it (Homer-Dixon 2006, Lovelock 2006). Journalist Melanie Phillips, for instance, suggests that the 'collapse of social order is a spiritual sickness' (Phillips 2005).

'Disillusionment' and 'disenfranchisement' are the new buzzwords for our beleaguered inner cities, socially strained townscapes, and isolated and abandoned villages. Dystopia is in the air. Stories of teenage violence on the streets are elevated to the top of the political agenda alongside reports of community fragmentation, family breakdown, the decline in social mores, racial tension and a general lack of trust in social interaction. Newspaper reports dwell on the problematic nature of interpersonal relations, from the enforced isolation of private car journeys to the decline and fall of the corner shop.

The so-called crises in local communities, virtual communities or ethnic communities are frequently discussed in economic, cultural and legalistic terms, but are increasingly given a psychological or pathological explanation. The UNICEF report in early 2007, which concluded that British children are the most disadvantaged in the developed world (UNICEF 2007), was taken as further evidence of society's loss of direction and reinforced a sense of political failure to tackle longstanding social problems. Related to this sense of failure is the perceived irrelevance of the political parties and a palpable sense of scepticism from the public at large.

With such a wealth of opinion on the nature and causes of these community issues, the government and its army of quangos show no lack of imagination about what to do about them. From anti-social behaviour orders (ASBOs) to promoting local identity; from constraints on urban sprawl to positive discrimination; from segregation to integration;

all of these discussions have at their core the idea that society needs to be reconstituted through rebuilding community, creating 'active' citizens and encouraging participation. The Community Service Volunteers' 'Make A Difference Day', for example, is hoping to persuade more people to help rekindle community spirit by putting together 'how-to' guides for potential volunteers, with suggestions such as baking fair-trade cookies and delivering them to older neighbours. Another guide, entitled *How to Knit Your Family Together*, shows people how families can knit blankets as a way of spending time together. While millions of pounds are spent on this kind of tosh, unsurprisingly there seems to be little sign of public enthusiasm for it.

The problem is that while the desire for people to be engaged members of their communities is a sensible one – especially among commentators and policy makers – the laboured 'engagement strategies' on offer are rather limited and patronising. Formal targets for greater participation are seldom accompanied by questions about what one is participating *in*, while official volunteering initiatives seem less about good will, and more about raising the volunteer's self-esteem. Participation is everything; content, nothing. Grassroots or genuinely organic community associations are often treated with suspicion, or 'channelled' by the imposition of third party intervention, often aimed at changing or directing people's behaviour.

So, it seems that the parameters of the discussion are set: by popular acknowledgement, community is either under threat or has collapsed already and most commentators want to reinstate it. The debate, such that it is, revolves around how best to do this. In America, Barack Obama wants to play a part in 'constructing communities' while Hillary Clinton

HOW (GOVERNMENT AND
BACKGROUND

is worried about 'fractured communities'. Back in Britain, Gordon Brown insists that immigrants should perform community work before being granted citizenship, and the Archbishop of Canterbury has suggested that sharia law would improve community relations. The only thing that links these examples is the sense of cultural desperation and political trepidation felt by the speaker and the establishment bodies that they represent. For despite an apparent consensus that rebuilding communities is an essential aim for twenty-first-century politics, with hundreds of technical agencies trying to implement it, there are no clear ideas about what they are doing ... or even what 'community' really means.

For example, UK Communities Secretary Hazel Blears has announced a £50 million, ten-point action plan to promote community cohesion. It includes a Citizenship Survey to assess and define the problem that it was set up to address; and a cohesion web-based 'one-stop shop' where you can develop 'cohesion policies or respond to cohesion issues'. It will include 'new cohesion impact tests ... a useful tool for "cohesion proofing" policies' (DCLG 2008). I'm sure that I am not alone in holding out little hope for the clarity of purpose in Blears's bureaucratic approach to social problems.

In this way, 'building community' has become a fetishistic issue for all tiers of government. It is just one of those management objectives that has to be ticked off. One local authority has identified the 'importance of the Community based Community Cohesion agenda and the role that Community Associations play in the Community' (Walsall Metropolitan Borough Council 2005). The Labour government encourages 'building the capacity of communities and community based organisations to deliver the informal, flexible services communities need and to engage in delivering change for communities' (Walsall Metropolitan Borough Council 2005). It seems that as long as they're talking about it – using the word – they are happy to believe that they are doing something positive.

However, with between 500,000 and 900,000 community groups operating, at all levels, in the UK (MacGillivray, Wadhams and Conaty 2001, NCVO 2006) among a population of 60.6 million people (38.36 million adults between 16 and 64 years of age) (Brown and Redgwell 2008) you might be forgiven for thinking that community organisation was in rude health. In fact it is true that the continued involvement of ordinary people in voluntary, charitable and community activity is testament to their desire to get things done. But the way that the debate is framed, as several of the essayists explore here, has nothing to do with *real* community development but concerns social engineering: an instrumental approach to engagement strategies. This book sets out to understand – and challenge – that strategy.

Take the authorities' response to the most basic participatory theatre known as the franchise: the vote. Disenfranchisement would indeed be a real problem but the contemporary trend for deliberative apathy by the erstwhile voting public appears to represent a rejection of the politics on offer (typified by the historically low 9.59 per cent voter turnout for the Liverpool Central local elections of May 2008). It suggests that while Margaret Hodge MP believes that the 'breakdown of community networks' (Hodge 2002) is a result of demoralisation, the answer is not simply to 'encourage' or cajole people into voting, but to address the void at the heart of politics that finds expression in people's disengagement. It's an old cliché, but if there was anything to vote for, people would vote. The record turnout of 48 per cent for the London mayoral election of 2008 shows that when people feel committed enough, they act. Imagine how engaged people could be with some real substance.

Unfortunately, in place of substance, we have a managerial approach to community engagement, which tends to undermine the very thing it seeks to create. One of the key recommendations from the government's (faintly Orwellian-sounding) Commission on Integration and Cohesion is that there needs to be a 'national programme of voluntary service for young people ... to contribute to their local area' (Commission on Integration and Cohesion 2008). Suddenly voluntarism becomes a compulsory obligation and community-spiritedness becomes a duty, rather than a choice. Implicit in the promotion of a state-sponsored (rather than voluntaristic) 'community' is a *desired* community response ... and a *wrong* community response:

> The state's role here is to support voluntary and community organisations that enable citizens to take responsibility and foster cooperation. But more than that – it is to foster a sense of ownership, pride and belonging in communities so that individuals take care of their surroundings and intervene when others do not – whether it is dropping litter or letting dogs foul pavements. (Miliband 2005)

In this sense, community engagement – a personal, private and often political choice to enter the social milieu – becomes public property. But can, or should, any government intervene in and attempt to recohere society or reinstate community values in this way? Although this question remains fundamentally unanswered, the UK government is still marching ahead with plans for a 'statutory "duty to involve"' (Blears 2007). This means, in essence, that by 2009 you will be obliged to be part of a community – whether you like it or not.

DIDNT HAPPEN. CHANGE OF GOVERNMENT

Indeed, the GCSE in Citizenship Studies imposes a requirement that students perform a 'community-based activity' (Edexcel 2003) which will contribute 40 per cent towards their final grade. If successful, a graduation ceremony will hopefully take place in a Town Hall, which the Commission believes will 'mark a young person's understanding of what it means to be a responsible citizen'. Sometimes you have to pinch yourself to remind yourself that they're talking about British communities, rather than the Chinese Young Pioneer movement. In fact, social commentator Charlie Leadbeater's vision of emerging web-based communities consciously harks back to 'pre-industrial forms of organisation: the commons, peer to peer working, community innovation and folk creativity' (Leadbeater 2008)

So what does community mean today? Is it a throwback to a romanticised lost era (Brierley 2004) (as Lynsey Hanley suggests in her book *Estates: An Intimate History* harking back to 'close knit communities' (Hanley 2007)); is it something that can be re-created? If communities are under siege as we are sometimes led to believe is government intervention necessarily a good idea? Or might such interference just undermine the informal bonds that make communities work in the first place?'

The Future of Community seeks to address the real issues in the debate about the much-reported death of community. The purpose of this book – a collection of think pieces designed to encourage a more critical engagement with the issues – is to challenge the blasé assumption that community is somehow naturally good; a moral absolute. Moreover, the notion that communities can be orchestrated into existence displays a casual disregard for the very thing that makes them special: communality – a voluntary association of interested parties.

To do that, *The Future of Community* questions the way the debate is being framed with 14 short, diverse essays, each one representing a critical examination of a specific aspect of the discussion. Some of the contributions will critique current policy while others will examine the forms that community takes today (in distinction to real and imagined communities from the recent, and not so recent, past.)

The topics weave various different strands together; from the new urbanist visions compared to the post-war ambitions; from the world of virtual communities to the panics about social networking. Chapters include analyses of the freedom of civic space versus the authoritarian response to interpersonal relationships; the politics of behaviour and the retreat into localism. A couple of positive vignettes – case studies on the historic integration of the Italian community in San Francisco and on the contemporary arrival of the Brazilian community in County Galway – exemplify some of the themes throughout the book.

The Future of Community concludes by arguing that the current understanding of community is not only inadequate, but counter-productive to the formation of real social solidarity. Instead this book offers a genuine alternative – one that embraces the notion of a voluntaristic, more assertive and ultimately more meaningful view of what it is to be an 'active' citizen in an 'active' community.

REFERENCES

Bannerman, L. and Ford, R. (2007) 'Police chief calls drinks industry to account for yob culture', *The Times*, 15 August

Blears, H. (2007) 'An action plan for community empowerment: building on success', Communities and Local Government, 19 October, p. 3

Brierley, N. (2004) 'In search of the good life', *New Statesman*, 13 December

Brown, S. and Redgwell, G. (2008) 'Key population and vital statistics: local and health authority areas population and vital statistics by area of usual residence in the United Kingdom, 2006', Office for National Statistics, Series VS No. 33, PPI No. 29, 2006 data, Palgrave Macmillan, pp. 12–13

Commission on Integration and Cohesion (2008) 'Building united and resilient communities – developing shared futures', Communities and Local Government, 25 April

Daily Mail (2006) 'Actor Everett labels Starbucks a "cancer"', 18 August

DCLG (2008) 'Guidance for local authorities on community cohesion contingency planning and tension monitoring', Department for Communities and Local Government, May, p. 26

Diamond, J. (2005) *Collapse: How Societies Choose to Fail or Succeed*, Viking Books

Edexcel (2003) 'Edexcel GCSE in Citizenship Studies. Short Course (3280): First Examination 2003', August, p. 14

Hanley, L. (2007) *Estates: An Intimate History*, Granta

Hodge, M. (2002) 'The problem is alienation, not apathy', *Guardian*, 14 March

Homer-Dixon, T. (2006) *The Upside of Down: Catastrophe, Creativity, and the Renewal of Civilization*, Island Press

Leadbeater, C. (2008) *We-Think*, Chapter 2, on-line version, www.charlesleadbeater.net (accessed 24 June 2008)

Lovelock, J. (2006) *The Revenge of Gaia: Why the Earth Is Fighting Back – and How We Can Still Save Humanity*, Allen Lane

Lunts, D. (2003) 'Urban renaissance – fact or fiction?', Office of the Deputy Prime Minister, College of Estate Management, Reading, 4 March

MacGillivray, A., Wadhams, C. and Conaty, P. (2001) *Low Flying Heroes*, London, New Economics Foundation

Miliband, D. (2005) 'Building a modern social contract', speech to the 'Together We Can' Conference, London, 29 May

NCVO (2006) *The UK Voluntary Sector Almanac*, London

Phillips, M. (2005) Melaniephillips.com, 23 June (accessed 27 June 2008)

Putnam, R. (2001) *Bowling Alone: The Collapse and Revival of American Community*, Simon and Schuster

Russell, B. (2008) 'Protesters scale Parliament roof in anti-runway demo', *Independent*, 28 February

UNICEF (2007) 'Child poverty in perspective: an overview of child well-being in rich countries – a comprehensive assessment of the lives and well-being of children and adolescents in the economically advanced nations', Innocenti Research Centre, Report Card 7, United Nations Children's Fund

Walsall Metropolitan Borough Council (2005) 'Community Association funding', Working Group Report, Community Organisation, Leisure and Culture Scrutiny & Performance Panel, autumn

Winterson, J. (2007) 'Real shopping', *Guardian*, 8 December

Part I

In Search of Community

1

Faking Civil Society

Dave Clements

In the past couple of years or so we have seen the rise of what might be called a new participatory paradigm. Of course, it has been around for longer than that. As Ben Rogers – a fan of innovation in local government and a visiting fellow at the Institute for Public Policy Research – says, the drive for 'greater public involvement' in public services, and experiments with 'citizens' juries, deliberative polling, citizens' assemblies, e-democracy and participatory budgeting', have been going on since at least the mid-1990s (Rogers 2008). But it is only more recently that it has acquired the political significance that it now has. I want to explore why that is.

There is a wide-ranging involvement imperative at work today, not a grassroots movement but a Whitehall-led mission to 'rebuild community' and revitalise civil society, through participatory mechanisms. The Local Government White Paper, *Strong and Prosperous Communities* (DCLG 2006), requires that local authorities forge 'strong links' with their respective communities, e.g. forcing them to ballot residents before deciding on their priorities. As part of the Best Value regime, the Local Government and Public Involvement in

Health Act 2007 has imposed on local authorities a new 'duty to involve'.

I will argue that these developments are not as positive as they might seem. Overall, they have worrying implications for the workings of our democracy, for the kind of politics we can expect to see for the foreseeable future, and for the state of our communities. Up until now, cynics have been able to content themselves that such initiatives are ultimately of little consequence, and can happily be ignored. But now they are centre stage and set to undermine still further people's relationships with politics and with each other.

THE PARTICIPATORY PARADIGM

Geoff Mulgan, chair of the Carnegie UK Trust Inquiry into the Future of Civil Society in the UK and Ireland, recently confirmed a hunch of mine – whatever civil society is, you and I are not a part of it. Unless you belong to one of the 'charities, social enterprises and voluntary organisations' that he says make it up, that is. The rest of us only know 'disconnect', as the former prime minister's former head of policy likes to put it. Mulgan is also chair of Involve, 'a charity bringing together practitioners in democracy and public engagement' that sits alongside government vehicles like 'Together We Can' in the campaign to 'engage' us with each other in our communities and of course *with them*.

Mulgan has expressed his concern that there is a lack of 'shared public arenas where communities can deliberate about the future' (Mulgan 2007). He needn't have worried. As promised in the Green Paper, *The Governance of Britain*, the government launched its first citizens' juries last year.

According to newly anointed prime minister Gordon Brown, they would herald a new type of politics, 'engage citizens in active democracy' and create 'better relationships between government and the people' (Panton 2007).

James Panton, a lecturer in politics at St John's College, Oxford, is sceptical. He thinks the new participatory paradigm is indicative of a managerial political class desperate to engage with the electorate as an end in itself. In the process, it seems to me, they are creating an almost seamless political discourse between civil renewal and a strategy meant to counter their own keenly felt estrangement from 'the people'. '[T]here is an appearance of democracy because the process is discursive', he argues, but 'the contours of the debate have been established in advance'. Participants are patronised and disempowered by the experts appointed to mediate the 'debate', in the hope that the 'right' conclusions are reached by all, he explains.

One contributor to this book, Suzy Dean, in a review of *Participation Nation: Reconnecting Citizens to the Public Realm* (2007), published by Involve, describes such participatory mechanisms and consultation initiatives as 'coercive participation'. '[W]hen the agenda is already set', she says, 'people's sense of apathy regarding public life is reaffirmed rather than challenged' (Dean 2008). Rather like putting a cross against the name of the least offensive candidate after an uninspiring election campaign, it can be an empty gesture, only reinforcing one's alienation from public life.

The simple fact is that citizens' juries and their like are neither able to breathe life into politics and public life, nor re-engage people in their communities. This is because they themselves are borne out of the very failure of politics that has given rise to so-called apathy in the first place. Unlike the institutions that went before them they are not able to mediate people's lives. They have no substantive social base and no wider legitimacy in the community. More worrying for me is that for all its vacuity, the participatory paradigm contains within it a set of assumptions about what people are like, what they are capable of 'engaging' with, and ultimately about what's good for them. The content of the deliberations of those first citizens' juries (i.e. health, crime and children) spoke volumes about how low our political leaders have sunk. This new deliberative politics can only contend with that which immediately impacts at a gut-level, that which worries the concerned citizen, the anxious parent, the worried-well, the fearful resident.

So what of petitions as a less mediated way of engaging in 'direct democracy', as an opportunity for people to say what they think about various issues, rather than being fed with the emotive 'pet' issues of the day, and prodded to make the appropriate affective response?

As Martyn Perks explains in his discussion of virtual communities in Chapter 8, the government's apparent enthusiasm for e-democracy seemed to wane early in 2007, when 1.8 million signatories to a government petition on congestion charging declared themselves opposed. When they met to discuss the matter, MPs were clearly rattled by the undermining of their own position, but also by such a naked expression of the popular will. Tony Wright MP, chair of the public administration select committee, was rather belittling of respondents' mere 'registering of dislike' of government policy. Another described the whole business as 'patronising, manipulative and sinister'. Fellow committee member, Kelvin Hopkins, went so far as to describe the petition as Hitleresque, courting the kind of right-wing populism that could 'whip up war fervour' (Tempest 2007).

There is a good argument that the rise of politics by petition, the bypassing of the ballot box and the undermining of representative democracy it implies, are nothing to be celebrated. But this is not it. The contempt for the idea that ordinary people are entitled to give their opinion, or even vent their frustrations however they see fit – whether it be via a petition, or by voting BNP – is underscored by a profound fear of the masses. Perhaps for this reason, and given the farce of the congestion charging e-petition, you might think the political class would steer well clear of petitions altogether.

On the contrary. Hazel Blears has proposed that councils should be required to respond to any petition signed by 250 or more of their residents, or by 1 per cent of the local population. This is in accordance with the new 'councillor's call to action' clause in the Local Government and Public Involvement in Health Act 2007. Blears (DCLG 2007b) proclaimed in a speech launching these new powers:

> Governments are elected to serve the people, and that applies locally as well as nationally. New petition powers would put more influence, power and control in the hands of communities, leading to greater action to tackle their concerns and improving the health of our local democracy.

You might argue, on the other hand, that this eagerness to put the rightful responsibilities of central and local government 'in the hands of communities' is not a democratic act, but rather symptomatic of our exhausted political culture. That the political elite should resort to asking us for ideas rather than proposing something of their own is not, after all, something to celebrate. It seems to me that this dearth of substance at the political centre is not unrelated to the official interest in the wider disconnect in our communities described by Mulgan.

The consequences of this 'interest' though are as likely as not to lead to further fragmentation rather than to re-connect individuals in their communities. For instance, as with citizens' juries, in the absence of anything else, Blears is rather keen on petitions that connect with people's anxieties – whether it's run-down streets, anti-social drinkers, installing streetlamps in run-down estates, or designing out 'blind corners' on parks and estates where unsavoury types congregate. Indeed, I would argue that the problem of political legitimacy – a lack of ideas and a failure of leadership – is being projected onto an already anxious society, and played out through a divisive communities agenda.

WE'RE ALL VOLUNTEERS NOW

This is particularly apparent in the political class's enthusiasm for volunteering. The government has made volunteering a central plank of its engagement strategy, as a way of rebuilding communities and a sense of civic duty. Without a hint of irony, it has now deemed volunteering virtually compulsory for aspiring *active* citizens. 2005 was the Year of the Volunteer. There is a Volunteering Week, and a Volunteering Day, and something called Make a Difference Day. Last year, the prime minister pledged to celebrate community champions and create a 'good neighbour MBE' to recognise the good work of volunteers (Branigan 2007).

Opposition leader, David Cameron, has been described as 'obsessed with volunteering' as a means of 'restoring civility' and rediscovering notions of 'mutual responsibility' in the belief that this is what 'transforms local communities for the better' (Newland 2007). Julia Neuberger, Liberal Democrat peer and chair of the Commission on the Future of Volunteering, looks forward to 'a society where volunteering is part of our DNA, so that by giving time we enrich our own lives and those of others' (Commission on the Future of Volunteering 2008). The ambitions of the Commission and the purpose behind initiatives such as Volunteering Week are to create a kinder, more connected society, and to promote volunteering as a 'form of civic engagement', she says.

An understanding of this vogue for volunteering in official circles is important if we are to have a richer understanding of the participatory paradigm. It shows what happens when the 'mechanisms' of which the Mulgan-ites are so fond are temporarily abandoned as the agenda moves into the midst of communities. Because for all this encouragement of individuals to participate in community life, to help needy others and in turn build a new society; the unmediated nature of the real world of relationships runs counter to the suspicious and fearful disposition we are encouraged to adopt towards each other, by the distrustful state. For all the fanfare surrounding the importance of volunteering, in practice the government has done all it can to institutionalise a culture of suspicion that can only put off those wishing to volunteer.

During Volunteering Week last year, a survey found that 13 per cent of men who didn't volunteer to work with children feared being branded a paedophile if they did. Following the passing of the Safeguarding Vulnerable Groups Act 2006, which ensured the massive extension of vetting procedures, 17 per cent specifically said they were put off by the prospect of having to undergo a criminal records check (Ives 2007).

This is indicative of a culture of suspicion that is also affecting relations between adults in the community. Neuberger has expressed her concern that 'no touch' protocols prevent volunteers in the care sector from bathing and feeding elderly and disabled people. '[I]n the present climate we are automatically suspicious of people wanting to visit nursing homes and care homes on a casual, uninvited basis', she says (Neuberger 2005: 48).

TERMS OF ENGAGEMENT

Just looking after someone that you happen to know, or helping out at the local community centre, has been politicised and turned into something else. But as Neuberger recognises, despite her advocacy for its wider significance, 'volunteering is often its own reward' (Neuberger 2007). Even those, like Neuberger, who are profoundly concerned about the hurdles put in the way of volunteers – and the impact that suspicion of their motives has on their valuable work in the community – are not immune to the pervasive culture of mistrust on which paedophile panics and rumours of elder abuse thrive.

The uncertainty about what volunteers working as football coaches or as care workers can and cannot do in their interactions with children, the elderly or adults with special needs is poisonous and stifling of normal adult relations with children and with vulnerable adults. Indeed, it is more pervasive even than that, colouring the way we all relate to each other in our everyday lives. The miserable view of what human beings do to each other is commonly held in official circles – and it is rarely treated with the contempt it deserves. This is because it speaks to a profound anxiety about even the most basic of informal relations.

This fearful individuation has its origins in the collapse of the old politics of left and right, and the failing legitimacy of social institutions from the Church of England to the trade unions, that once bound us together (or at either side of an ideological divide) and helped us make sense of the world and our place in it. But can the state rebuild community or revitalise civil society, or should it steer well clear? My contention is that it is doing more damage than good in its efforts to secure its own legitimacy, and to find a new rationale in the often petty politics of community.

REALLY 'ACTIVE' CITIZENS

Despite this underlying anxiety that pervades society, and official attempts to rediscover a sense of purpose through the community agenda, it is perhaps worth mentioning that on account of living in communities, we inevitably *participate* in them too. This might seem like an obvious point to make but in the fretting over community on the one hand, and the exaggeration of the extent of volunteering on the other, it is in danger of being overlooked.

Community is made of the casual and more intimate bonds that we make and remake every day. But this does not mean, as some claim, that 22 million of us are volunteers, on the basis that many do something vaguely selfless at least once a year. Indeed the politics of participation, of which the official volunteering push is a part, is undermining that which it seeks to bolster – i.e. the *voluntary* relations of trust and good will that we all enter into without the need for official encouragement, but out of a 'sense of community' that apparently eludes the authorities.

Countervailing trends mean that political and cultural imperatives are strangling the 'giving' nature that we all possess to a greater or lesser extent. Where people fail to engage – with each other or with the wider world of politics – there is reason to believe that this has less to do with apathy, or even antipathy necessarily, and more to do with the kinds of misanthropic goings-on sanctioned by the authorities. By exploiting people's fears about each other and by constructing a politics to fit, people's estrangement from each other is confirmed and codified.

This 'tendency to believe the worst in one another', as Zoë Williams (2007) puts it, is not conducive to the construction of Blears's 'confident communities'. Williams argues compellingly that if only the government could bring itself to trust people to get on with their lives they might find a 'seam of civic duty' running right through our communities. I think she is right. Why is it that those who claim to want to re-engage us and rebuild our communities are also the ones that seem to be so intent on sowing the seeds of distrust?

To engage people in this way by exploiting their fears, and by putting them off 'getting involved' in their communities by institutionalising a culture of mistrust, is indicative of a political elite that wants to engage us but has nothing to engage us *with* but the politics of fear. We need to rediscover the potential of politics and ideas to transform communities for the better, but this can only be achieved by cultivating a sense of ourselves as robust and truly active citizens able to work together to that end. Only then can we build a really civil society.

REFERENCES

Branigan, T. (2007) 'Honour ordinary heroes, says PM', *Guardian*, 25 July

Commission on the Future of Volunteering (2008) 'Volunteering must be a part of society's DNA', press release, 28 January

DCLG (2006) *Strong and Prosperous Communities*: Local Government White Paper

DCLG (2007a) Local Government and Public Involvement in Health Act

DCLG (2007b) 'Petition power kicks off new year of community action', press release, 27 December

Dean, S. (2008) 'Down with coercive participation', *spiked*, 10 January, www.spiked-online.com/index.php?/site/article/4257 (accessed 24 June 2008)

Ives, J. (2007) 'Suspicious minds deter male volunteers', *Society Guardian*, 1 June

Mulgan, G. (2007) 'Civil engineering', *Guardian*, 24 October

Neuberger, J. (2005) *The Moral State We're In: A Manifesto for a 21st Century Society*, HarperCollins

Neuberger, J. (2007) 'Unsung heroes', *Society Guardian*, 5 June

Newland, M. (2007) 'All my family wanted to do was help. So why make it so hard?', *Observer*, 17 June

Panton, J. (2007) 'Government by the people for the people?', *Policy Review*, December

Rogers, B. (2008) 'Innovation made easy', *Guardian*, 30 January

Tempest, M. (2007) 'E-petitions could undermine democracy, MPs warned', 8 May, www.guardian.co.uk/society/2007/mar/08/epublic.egovernment/ (accessed 5 May 2008)

Williams, Z. (2007) 'Britain's on a civility binge', *Guardian*, 9 May

E-PETITIONS HAVE BECOME A VALUABLE TOOL TO GET ISSUES OF CONCERN DEBATED IN PARLIAMENT

2
A Green Unpleasant Land

Alastair Donald

A decade ago, Jonathon Porritt, chair of the government's Sustainable Development Commission, suggested that 'sustainable development and community participation must go hand in hand. You can't have one without the other' (Porritt 1999: iii). In the time since, the mandate for what the Sierra Club[1] called 'building environmental community' has taken root, and claims for the community benefits of environmentalism are rife. Matthew Taylor, chief executive of the Royal Society of the Encouragement of Arts (RSA) and ex-New Labour adviser, suggests climate change offers a 'fascinating opportunity to interweave stories of action at the individual, community, national and international levels' (Taylor 2008). Like ex-environment secretary David Miliband who views climate change as the 'mass-mobilising issue of our age' (Miliband 2006c), Taylor sees a rallying point: environmentalism has become the focus around which 'progressives' aim to reclaim social ambition and develop the institutions of a 'new collectivism' (Taylor 2008).

This chapter presents a challenge to these lofty sounding claims. The attempt to build 'environmental communities' is actually a far more pragmatic project – one that responds to New Labour's own uncertainty and lack of purpose, and its apparent inability to generate any commonly held principles or shared moral commitments. As Miliband put it during his time as minister for communities, the search is on for the 'decent values around which we can all agree', values that could form the basis for a 'modern Social Contract' (Miliband 2005). Others in this book point out the limitations of the 'shared responsibilities' and 'mutual respect' of a social contract. Here, I look at how the 'rights and responsibilities' agenda has taken an environmental turn.

It should come as little surprise that environmentalism has become central to the debate around communities. While Friends of the Earth and others continue to protest darkly about non-environmentalists sowing 'sources of confusion and denial' (Juniper 2007: 27), there is no doubt that the assumptions and beliefs of environmentalism have become dominant. Some take a distinctly cynical view of political parties that urge 'vote Blue, go Green' (Cameron 2006), or who profess to have become a 'greener shade of red' (Miliband 2007). Yet, if the former view disregards the long tradition of ecology within sections of the upper and middle classes (Bramwell 1994), the latter steadfastly ignores the conversion of Labour to the new ethos. A glance at the eco-mission statements of numerous businesses and institutions ranging from Marks and Spencer[2] to the Church of England[3] is enough to confirm the mainstreaming of the environmental message.

With the ritualistic daily presentation of 'evidence' on a changing climate, the message is actually quite hard to avoid. Nature is extracting a heavy price for our irresponsible behaviour is the core script; act now or pay the price for slothful ways. In one typically apocalyptic tale (based on an EU report), global warming precipitates security issues for Europe 'ranging from energy wars to mass migration, failed states and political radicalisation' (Traynor 2008). As the four horsemen ride rapidly into the purview of some people, the imperative for taking action is presented as a self-evident truth. (Marks and Spencer is typical, presenting their Plan A 'eco-plan' for ethical trading as the only way to do business. 'There's no plan B' they assert.[4])

If the *need* to act is now beyond debate, ideas about *how* we should deal with environmental problems differ markedly from the past, and illustrate one way the discussion impacts on communities. In the past, environmental problems would often be resolved at the level of society. Applying resources and creative impetus could lead to technological solutions to problems, or at least help us adapt to new situations. If we wanted to live in neighbourhoods in attractive but flood-prone riverside locations, we designed flood barriers; cars may have polluted the city air, but by improving the design of engines we could enhance mobility and hence extend our social networks – all while air quality improved. Broadly speaking, the efforts of society to grapple with environmental dilemmas did not mean curtailing the freedoms and choices as to how we lived.

Today the opposite seems to be the case. Environmental action revolves around the idea of 'mitigation' in which the dominant theme is that we all should moderate what we do and what we want to achieve. Ambitious construction projects to allow us to inhabit flood plains are out, and communities are expected to settle for less attractive locations. Instead of technological improvements to mobility, we are urged to travel less, and find contentment by working, shopping and socialising locally. Each member of a community works out where they can make sacrifices, lower their environmental impact and live more sustainably. Such is our consumption of resources stress the WWF, that if everyone wanted to live as we do in England we would need three planets just to survive.[5]

There is considerable pressure to embrace this new ethos and become an active participant in environmental actions. Indeed significant resources have been invested in mechanisms and forums through which communities are 'engaged' around environmental activities (for an overview see Centre for Sustainable Energy and Community Development Xchange 2007). Community Action for Energy[6] stimulates and supports action to engage communities with sustainable energy; the Community Recycling Network[7] regenerates deprived communities; and the Community Composting Network[8] creates a sense of community ownership/civic pride. While too numerous to mention here, many initiatives are motivated by the belief that 'communities are well placed to influence individual behaviour' and therefore that 'community engagement can directly and transparently translate into measurable and sustainable behaviour' (Centre for Sustainable Energy and Community Development Xchange 2007: 4). That such explicit exercises in social engineering seldom provoke comment suggests how commonplace official intervention in shaping personal behaviour has become.

There is also considerable emphasis on communities to *demonstrate* their involvement through advertising their eco credentials, often with ostentatious displays of their actions. Indeed a veritable industry has grown in the design and arrangement of the various accoutrements and paraphernalia of ethical living. We walk around carrying bags that advertise

'I'm not a plastic bag', meaning 'I'm not the problem' while pointing the finger at those who are. Conspicuous cycle lanes weave their way through otherwise quiet neighbourhoods. In fact demonstrating our credentials often seems more important than the environmental benefits of the action itself. Windmills hoisted high onto roofs have little or no useable energy generation capacity (Taylor 2005/2006) and appear designed more to send out the 'right' message to others. This self-conscious display is mimicked in bottle banks placed in prominent neighbourhood locations. One report dismissively suggests 'it would be more economically efficient and environmentally friendly to throw the bottles away' (*The Economist* 2007). So, if many environmental activities count for little in their own terms, why the desire to make such a display?

The premium placed on sending out the right eco message suggests an important feature of environmental action is about displaying our values – demonstrating what we stand for, and that we are in agreement with the new set of communal ethics. David Miliband has suggested the importance of discovering how 'social order can be created in an age where values of individualism and meritocracy have replaced deference and hierarchy' (Miliband 2005). Advertising that we care about the environment and that we accept the strictures and accompanying moral codes seems to offer the prospect of a display of shared moral commitments in society. Purchasing ethically; consuming responsibly; scrutinising CO_2 emissions; all place values and an ethical outlook firmly at the centre of individual and community life. And for those not minded to engage with the new norm? Well, as the RCA's Matthew Taylor asserts, 'refusing to do something about cutting your carbon footprint means you are obeying the norms of individualism and materialism over those of sustainability and collective responsibility' (Taylor 2007).

It is plain that the new ethical values have permeated widely, and codes of conduct around ethical behaviour and the new etiquette of 'reduce, reuse, recycle' have proved very successful in shaping beliefs and attitudes. While we might not all be willing to put the hours in on a daily basis to purchase ethically, sort our garbage or switch off the standby, eco-slackers clearly feel the need to keep up with the green Joneses next door. According to one survey 'eco-guilt' now means many of us are even prepared to lie about our actions to maintain the image that we've 'done our bit' (Smith 2007). Yet 'eco-guilt' seems a strange foundation for building a 'new collectivism'. A community of guilt, blame and shame represents community in name only, and will surely prove less successful at creating a sense of purpose about the future than a consensus for moderating our individual behaviour in accordance with the new environmentally codified stipulations.

As if aware of this contradiction, discussion occasionally breaks out as to 'profound questions' such as the balance between 'paternalism and individual freedom' (Miliband 2006b). Yet the authoritarian dynamic around environmentalism is clear, and ferments evermore chaperoning of behaviour, and a growing intolerance of those unwilling to bow to behavioural change mandates. A survey from the Norwich Union (Smith 2007) found over half the respondents viewed 'unethical living' as taboo as drink driving. With 'taboo' eco-behaviour deemed socially unacceptable, there could be little surprise that New Labour's un-environmental activities committee declared 'the failure to recycle is essentially an example of anti-social behaviour' (Miliband 2006a).

Indeed the standards of eco-behaviour are increasingly being set by officialdom. While domestic recycling makes little sense in terms of the efforts required and the results obtained (Earnshaw 2007), etiquette for disposing of domestic rubbish has become formalised in law along with fines for dissenters, or even anyone just unfortunate enough to place waste in the wrong bin. Southwark Council in south London introduced residents to its plans with a letter headlined, 'Recycling the easy way ... or the hard way' (Southwark Council 2007). The hard way it transpires is as menacing as it sounds with 'recycling enforcement officers' checking bins and monitoring compliance, and fines of £75, possible criminal charges and moral opprobrium for those failing to meet the mark.

The predilection for regulating behaviour around environmental actions seems distinctly at odds with the aim of creating active citizens – presumably who should be trusted to determine their own priorities and those for the community. Yet the environmental community agenda clearly illustrates the way that a genuine sense of active citizenship is inimical to the government's paternalistic agenda for community. Instead of working together to exercise genuine choice, communities are treated as rather feckless, and in need of guidance to ensure that predetermined priorities are put into action. The discussion around recycling is a case in point. Having introduced targets for the amount of rubbish recycled – a decision that was entirely bureaucratic and for which no popular mandate existed – the ongoing failure to meet targets is unsurprising. Yet instead of recognising that the problem revolves around the demand that communities change their behaviour to meet with externally imposed expectations, the government instead blames communities themselves, and bemoans the 'power of inertia'. Ironically this serves to further undermine genuine choice. As one report for DEFRA suggests, 'if government is to encourage change in those that are currently highly apathetic or reluctant, it needs to ... "remove the get out clause"'(Policy Studies Institute 2007).

One result is that the onus to measure and audit what we do is becoming ever-present. The proposal to issue carbon credit cards (Miliband 2006c) as part of a carbon trading system illustrates this well. Under this system everyone assesses the carbon implications of each activity to ascertain how far our personal emissions allowance stretches, and ascertain what we might trade with neighbours or friends. Not only are we saddled with the tedious job of counting and accounting for everything we do, but what might have been spontaneous decisions and interactions become prescribed and community relations formalised and managed through a technical trading framework.

Unsurprisingly, attempts to develop communal values through this sort of imposed managerial framework only serve to damage the way neighbourly relations evolve. In the absence of genuine freedom of choice, actions rendered subservient to the greater purpose of the new carbon codes increase suspicion, and seem likely to prompt disharmony rather than imbue communities with a genuinely communal sprit. After Southwark introduced its recycling initiative, the prospect of being fined concentrated some minds on the possibility that neighbours or passers-by might be tempted to put rubbish in bins other than their own. Instead of potential allies, the danger is that others in the community become latent anti-social elements, just waiting to drop the wrong sort of rubbish in our wheelie bins. Externally enforced priorities can encourage a more hostile and intolerant view of one's neighbours.

Environmentalists have been particularly keen to assert the community enhancing powers of taking production back into the community itself, for example by decentralising energy supply to community level (Greenpeace 2005). In the Budenburg Haus Projekte, the trendy Norman Foster-designed apartment block in Altrincham, Cheshire, an 'off-grid' community energy system links residents through an internal cable TV system (Willis 2006). Not only are instant updates available concerning one's own energy consumption, but also usage can be compared with that of neighbours. Yet when Neighbourhood Watch becomes Carbon Watch, communities exist only as carbon creators, with each of us monitoring others against targets for carbon efficiency, and open to condemnation should we deviate from the suggested optimum sustainable lifestyles.

While it is difficult to escape the conclusion that there is truly a need to encourage communities to stand up to some of these insidious proposals, the lauded 'new collectivism' is centred upon precisely these types of localised initiatives. With universal provision now thought to be 'disempowering' to communities, decentralising is celebrated as a means of fostering democratic renewal, and presenting 'real opportunities for local political leadership' (Greenpeace 2005). In all seriousness, Neal Lawson, chair of Compass, argues that *Grid 2.0: The Next Generation* – a short pamphlet on decentralised energy supply – is one of the 'best political pamphlets' in a long time (Lawson 2006). Proclamations as to the revolutionary potential of community heating systems, endorsed by the likes of the former London Mayor Ken Livingstone (2005: 1), are seldom questioned. Yet surely there can be few better illustrations of a redundant political culture than claims for the progressive benefits of connecting communities through bio-mass boiler systems or other forms of decentralised infrastructure?

At the forefront of the emerging localist production initiatives is the Transition Network[9] consisting of 36 communities ranging from urban Brixton to rural Lostwithiel, each responding to the threat of 'peak oil' by planning an 'energy descent'. Central to the transition is the desire to 'relocalise' all aspects of community life to build 'community resilience'. Arrangements are being made to produce food and energy within the community; key goods and building materials will be locally sourced; local ownership of businesses is encouraged, as is increasing the proportion of local workers. Even alternative local currencies such as the Totnes Pound have been developed.[10]

Yet for all the claims of a life that is 'more fulfilling, more socially connected and more equitable',[11] the idea of 'community resilience' represents a withdrawal from wider society, and a retreat from the opportunities for engagement in the wider world as socially equitable partners. It merely operates as a defence mechanism against the outside world, suggesting not only that we are no longer capable of engaging with it, but that the confines of community life are as good as it gets. By confining what we do to organising our survival on a localised basis, the likes of Transition Network end up downgrading the creative side of human beings and underplaying what we are capable of achieving. Like it or not, they undermine the idea that society can make progress towards a materially and culturally richer future.

Indeed, one of the most remarkable aspects of the rise of environmental communities is the extent to which ideas are upheld as radical rather than exposed for their deeply conservative outlook on life. Rob Holden, the eco guru and designer who presented Channel 4's 2007 reality TV series *Dumped*, earned kudos for the 'audacious' idea that communities might derive some valid insights to life from contestants spending three weeks living off scraps in a landfill site. One participant celebrated the manner in which such restrictive circumstances had helped generate 'a tight knit community' (Holland 2007).

In reality there was little evidence of 'community' on display among the self-righteous majority of bickering contestants. But perhaps that's not surprising. Arguing that 'nappies, syringes, rotten veg' revealed 'the dark side of consumerism' (Holland 2007), one of the contestants clearly illustrates the way that the moralistic monitoring of consumption results in new arbitrary criteria with which to judge the habits and personalities of friends, colleagues and neighbours – while at the same time allowing those who have 'done their bit' to radiate contentment at their own 'eco friendly' behaviour. Such a level of narcissism seems to militate against meaningful social interaction, suggesting our ambitions are more directed to finding satisfaction in the ethics of our own personal behaviour than developing successful relations with others. As Richard Sennett (1977) notes in *The Fall of Public Man*, this type of self-absorption undermines a more rewarding form of relations within the public sphere, and certainly cannot signify a 'new collectivism' that can actively reclaim social ambition.

The view that communities should exercise and celebrate puritan-style self-restraint has the potential to be deeply damaging. Everyone from Thom Yorke, rockstar and Friends of the Earth 'ambassador', to Prince Charles, heir to the royal fortune, seem in a rush to outline their version of an austere future, with a common theme that a wartime footing and rationing is inevitable (Yorke 2007, Windsor 2007). Rebuilding

Jerusalem around environmental communities seems to revolve around a return to the straitened circumstances of a wartime economy, when, Dig for Victory-style, communities grew their own food and generally had to make do and mend. Little wonder that, according to one communities minister, it will be communal allotments that help usher in the social networks of the future, and which will take pride of place at the centre of community life in the government's new Eco Towns (Andrews 2008).

As a vision for communities, the aspiration for a better life has been demeaned by the fact that not only is community life being reduced to obsessing over personal consumption and disposal activities, but we are becoming tied up in ever greater amounts of regulation. Both constrict our freedoms to form meaningful communities. In order to build communities successfully, human beings must be seen as central positive actors. Instead, environmentalists identify humanity – and therefore those making up the community– as the problem. Who knows, it may just be that in the process of making that argument, we might create the space in society for the emergence of a sense of what unites us.

NOTES

1. Sierra Club, 'Building environmental community: neighbours together', www.sierraclub.org/community/ (accessed 1 April 2008)
2. Marks and Spencer, http://plana.marksandspencer.com/?action=PublicPillarDisplay (accessed 1 April 2008)
3. Church of England: Shrinking the Footprint, www.shrinkingthefootprint.cofe.anglican.org/church40.php (accessed 1 April 2008)

4. Marks and Spencer, http://plana.marksandspencer.com/
   ?action=PublicPillarDisplay (accessed 1 April 2008)
5. WWF UK – One Planet Future Campaign, www.wwf.org.uk/
   oneplanet/ophome.asp (accessed 1 April 2008)
6. Community Action for Energy, http://lowcarboncommunity.org/
   communities/ (accessed 1 April 2008)
7. Community Recycling Network, www.crn.org.uk (accessed 1 April
   2008)
8. Community Composting Network, www.communitycompost.org/
   news/ccinterimreport.pdf (accessed 1 April 2008)
9. Transition Towns, www.transitiontowns.org/ (accessed 1 April
   2008)
10. Transition Town Totnes (2008), http://totnes.transitionnetwork.
    org/totnespound/home (accessed 1 April 2008)
11. Transition Towns Primer (version 25), http://transitionnetwork.
    org/Primer/TransitionInitiativesPrimer.pdf (accessed 1 April
    2008)

REFERENCES

Andrews, K. (2008) 'Our built heritage: the way ahead', speech to
'New Buildings in Old Places' conference, 31 January, www.
communities.gov.uk/speeches/corporate/ourbuiltheritage (accessed
1 April 2008)

Bramwell, A. (1994) *The Fading of the Greens: The Decline of
Environmental Politics in the West*, New Haven, Yale University
Press

Cameron, D. (2006) 'Cameron vows "green revolution"', *BBC News
24*, 18 April, http://news.bbc.co.uk/1/hi/uk_politics/4917516.stm
(accessed 1 April 2008)

Centre for Sustainable Energy (CSE) and Community Development
Xchange (CDX) (2007) 'Mobilising individual behaviour change
through community initiatives: lessons for climate change', www.
defra.gov.uk/environment/climatechange/uk/individual/pdf/study1-
0207.pdf (accessed 1 April 2008)

Earnshaw, M. (2007) 'Recycling: reducing waste or a waste of time?', *Battle of Ideas*, www.battleofideas.org.uk/index.php/2008/battles/951/ (accessed 1 April 2008)

The Economist (2007) 'The price of virtue', 7 June, www.economist.com/opinion/displaystory.cfm?story_id=9302727 (accessed 1 April 2008)

Greenpeace (2005) *Decentralising Power: An Energy Revolution for the 21st Century*, London, Greenpeace, www.greenpeace.org.uk/MultimediaFiles/Live/FullReport/7154.pdf (accessed 1 April 2008)

Holland, J. (2007) 'This mess is all too real', *The London Paper*, 31 August

Juniper, T. (2007) 'Creating a climate for participation; global warming, the public and the search for elusive solutions' in Creasy, S. (ed.) *Participation Nation: Reconnecting Citizens to the Public Realm*, London, Creative Commons, http://83.223.102.125/involvenew/mt/archives/blog_37/Involve%20Participation%20Nation.pdf (accessed 1 April 2008)

Lawson, N. (2006) 'Foreword' to *Grid 2.0: The Next Generation*, London, Green Alliance, www.ashdentrust.org.uk/PDFs/The%20Next%20Generation.pdf (accessed 1 April 2008)

Livingstone, K. (2005) 'Foreword' to *Decentralising Power: An Energy Revolution for the 21st Century*, London, Greenpeace, www.greenpeace.org.uk/MultimediaFiles/Live/FullReport/7154.pdf (accessed 1 April 2008)

Miliband, D. (2005) 'Building a modern social contract', Communities and Local Government Speech to 'Together We Can' conference, 28 June, www.neighbourhood.gov.uk/news.asp?id=1524 (accessed 1 April 2008)

Miliband, D. (2006a) 'Power devolved is energy released', DEFRA Speech to Local Government Association Annual Conference, Bournemouth, 4 July, www.defra.gov.uk/corporate/ministers/speeches/david-miliband/dm060704.htm (accessed 1 April 2008)

Miliband, D. (2006b) 'The great stink: towards an environmental contract', DEFRA Speech to the Audit Commission, 19 July, www.defra.gov.uk/corporate/ministers/speeches/david-miliband/dm060719.htm (accessed 1 April 2008)

Miliband, D. (2006c) 'Carbon "credit card" considered', *BBC News 24*, 11 December, http://news.bbc.co.uk/1/hi/uk_politics/6167671. stm (accessed 1 April 2008)

Miliband, D. (2007) 'A greener shade of red' in Pearce, N. and Margo, J. (eds) *Politics for a New Generation: The Progressive Moment*, London, Palgrave Macmillan

Policy Studies Institute (2007) 'A synthesis review of the public understanding research reports', www.defra.gov.uk/science/Project_ Data/DocumentLibrary/EV02065/EV02065_6902_FRP.pdf (accessed 1 April 2008)

Porritt, J. (1999) 'Foreword' to Warburton, D. (ed.) *Community and Sustainable Development: Participation in the Future*, London, Earthscan

Sennett, R. (1977) *The Fall of Public Man* (1993 edn) London, Faber and Faber

Smith, L. (2007) 'Eco slackers feel the need to keep up with the green Joneses', *The Times*, 24 August, http://women.timesonline.co.uk/tol/ life_and_style/women/the_way_we_live/article2317266.ece (accessed 1 April 2008)

Southwark Council (2007) 'Recycling the easy way. Recycling the hard way' leaflet, www.southwark.gov.uk/YourServices/environment/ RecyclingPages/theeasyway.html (accessed 1 April 2008)

Taylor, D. (2005/2006) 'Potential outputs from 1–2m dia. wind turbines', *Building for a Future*, winter, www.buildingforafuture. co.uk/winter05/30-58.pdf (accessed 1 April 2008)

Taylor, M. (2007) 'Pro-social behaviour: the future – it's up to us', www.rsa.org.uk/acrobat/pro-social_behaviour.pdf (accessed 1 April 2008)

Taylor, M. (2008) 'Why life is good', *New Statesman*, 3 January, www. newstatesman.com/200801030023 (accessed 1 April 2008)

Traynor, I. (2008) 'Climate change may spark conflict with Russia, EU told', *Guardian*, 10 March

Willis, R. (2006) *Grid 2.0: The Next Generation*, www.ashdentrust. org.uk/PDFs/The%20Next%20Generation.pdf (accessed 1 April 2008)

Windsor, C. (2007) 'Climate change fight is like war against Nazis', *USA Today*, www.usatoday.com/weather/climate/globalwarming/2007-05-01-prince-charles_N.htm (accessed 1 April 2008)

Yorke, T. (2007) quoted in McLean, C. 'Caught in the flash', *Guardian*, http://music.guardian.co.uk/omm/story/0,,2222272,00.html (accessed 1 April 2008)

3
Public Space:
Designing-in Community

Richard Williams

Public spaces have proliferated in Britain since the mid-1990s. Some have been refurbishments of existing spaces, such as the Trafalgar Square redevelopment completed by Norman Foster + Partners in 2002. But many were entirely new creations. The spate of new cultural facilities created with National Lottery assistance money in the late 1990s and early 2000s invariably included significant, and sometimes very large elements of public space. In one celebrated case, the Great Court of the British Museum, again by Foster + Partners, public space seemingly displaced the traditional display space of the museum. Here, in the largest single development in the museum's modern history, was a newly created gathering space, imagined in the tradition of Bloomsbury's Georgian squares. Its creation involved the literal evacuation of the old British Library. It was for many critics a symbolic displacement of educational and curatorial functions to the margins.

Trafalgar Square and the Great Court are two of the most high profile of public space projects of this time. But they represent a much wider tendency towards the sublimation of public space in British urbanism at the end of the twentieth century. You might think of the sustained investment in public space along the banks of the River Thames, which on the south side now provides a continuous stretch of public space from Westminster to Tower Bridge and beyond: virtually none of this existed as recently as 1980. Think of the expanse of high quality public space at Canary Wharf, now permanently thronged with fund managers on weekdays. Think of the reformed public areas around Paternoster or Finsbury Squares in the City. Outside of London, the tendency has been if anything more dramatic. Manchester has its Exchange and Great Northern Squares and a web of new public spaces in its Spinningfields development. Salford Quays has huge plazas around the Lowry arts centre, to be augmented still further by the arrival of the BBC. Leeds has its Millennium Square, Birmingham its Centenary Square and Brindleyplace, Sheffield, a new public quarter around its refurbished art gallery, and Cardiff new spaces around the site of the Welsh Assembly. Edinburgh, already awash with civic spaces, has a network of new pedestrian routes defining the redevelopment of its former Royal Infirmary. It would be hard not to notice these things, and think that Britain had undergone some kind of revolution as regards public space over the past decade.

These spaces vary a good deal of course. Trafalgar Square is a project of traffic management more than anything else. The work on London's South Bank has been incremental and low key, although the overall result is substantial. Leeds's Millennium Square is, by contrast with the above, a bombastic piece of contemporary architecture, a Yorkshire interpretation of Koolhaas. Yet in spite of the formal differences, it would be hard not to notice the consensus about these spaces, the widely held belief that they are good and right and that they should be encouraged, beliefs which have been institutionalised at all levels of government. Through such state-defined mechanisms as the Lottery, grants have been awarded to projects in part because of the extent to which they can be shown to revitalise the public realm. Almost every museum or gallery funded by Lottery money has also been a public space; sometimes, as in the case of the Great Court, the public space has almost seemingly displaced the museum.

What are the ideas that have made such a proliferation possible? Many are concepts of community. Here, for example, is Richard Rogers, Ken Livingstone's first design tsar. Writing in his polemic *Cities for a Small Planet*, he says that in the 'great public spaces of Europe', he feels 'part of the community of the city' (Rogers 1997: 15). It is here in these spaces, as well as more modest urban spaces, that 'citizenship is enacted'; it is 'glue that can bind an urban society' (Rogers 1996: 16). Here is Ken Livingstone justifying London's 100 Public Spaces project: 'Creating and managing high quality public spaces is essential to delivering an urban renaissance in London', he argues; 'new and revitalised public spaces can make a real difference to individual quality of life, community vitality and make London more liveable' (Greater London Authority 2002).

In different ways, Joseph Rykwert, Richard Sennett, and Oriol Bohigas have argued the same thing: that the city and its public space are coterminous, and that urban community is defined by urban public space (Rykwert 2000, Sennett 1994, Bohigas 1999). Their work strongly informs the present consensus. At the heart of all this is a set of key images of public spaces informing a set of beliefs about urban space in the western world: the Greek *agora* and its Roman adaptation, the *forum*, the space where citizens routinely met to perform citizenship and conduct business; the *campo* of medieval Siena, a space used to this day as the meeting point of public and private lives; the countless *paseos* of the Hispanic world, in which the eponymous social ritual is carried out; the grand nineteenth-century promenading spaces of (for example) the Galleria Vittorio Emmanuele in Milan, or St Mark's in Venice; the space of sanctioned protest on Speakers' Corner in Hyde Park, London; the network of informal social spaces created by accident more than by design in New York's Greenwich Village.

These images and ideas are surely familiar. They have passed into the realm of commonsense thinking, at which point they largely exist beyond criticism. The public spaces we have created and continue to create are simply what we do. They are no longer much reflected upon; they are rarely of themselves controversial, except perhaps at detail level as in the case of Trafalgar Square, when the scheme upset taxi drivers. We almost never hear arguments *against* the creation of new public spaces. Perhaps we should. Let me rehearse a few such arguments, or more specifically, against public space as a means of creating community.

First is a historical argument. In modern times, cities have rarely, if ever, created public spaces as a representation of community. They have barely even been expressions of democracy. Consider the reform of late nineteenth-century Paris under Baron Haussman. Its public spaces were meant primarily to secure military power, abolishing the medieval *quartiers* which housed the unruly lower orders. The new streets and squares are, if nothing else, a representation of class war on a grand scale. Consider the echoes of Haussman's Paris in Vienna, Rio de Janeiro, Buenos Aires, Berlin, Bucharest, even Moscow and Pyongyang, none of them democracies at the moment when they took an interest in the public realm. Consider Trafalgar Square, not as an expression of community, but of – as Rodney Mace argued – imperial power (Mace 1976). Consider therefore public space not as a representation of inclusiveness, but often, frankly, the reverse. The imperial spaces of nineteenth-century Europe are overt expressions of imperial power.

Second is a contradiction. The contemporary advocates of public space, including Livingstone, often cite with affection the appropriation of public spaces for protest. Trafalgar Square has long unofficially held this role. In the liberal mind, it is a place where London manifests itself as a progressive community, united in opposition to authoritarianism. It was the site of the long-running picket outside the South African embassy during the 1980s and the anti-poll tax riots of 1990, which played such a key part in the careers of Nelson Mandela and Margaret Thatcher respectively. These events showed the square at its fullest, at its most vibrant, yet they also show it at moments of confrontation with authority, whether that of the state of South Africa or the British government. Yet these activities, fundamentally anti-authoritarian, happened in spite of the official imagination, in spite of the square. That anti-authoritarian spirit cannot be meaningfully created now by authority itself – or if it is, then only as street theatre.

Third is the element of touristic fantasy. Much of the advocacy of public space invokes a public life on the southern European model. As I have argued elsewhere, this is an apparently inclusive state whose most representative physical expression might be the Spanish *paseo*, a form of ritualised public promenading along a set route at a commonly agreed time, interspersed with visits to cafés and other points of interest (Williams 2004: 82–106). This model is based on a very different social organisation to that commonly found in northern Europe and the United States. It is a model in which church and family assume a far greater importance than they do elsewhere, in which women are more firmly fixed in domestic roles, and in which – crucially – all or most social and economic functions are contained within a limited geographical area. Many new British public spaces produced in recent years have derived inspiration from such a model. Yet to hope to create a Mediterranean expression of community is not only misguided, when the social frameworks are so different, it may not even be desirable. The *paseo* – if I can cite that as representative of the Mediterranean city – constitutes a fundamentally affirmative view of urban life in which the participation in the public realm, the act of being-in-public, is expressive of a world order with God at the top. The being-in-public imagined by Livingstone and other latter-day advocates of the public realm formed in the Anglophone world of the 1960s is based on models of conflict and confrontation with authority; the two models of public life are based on wholly different assumptions.

Fourth is the tendency of public space to inhibit community as much as it may lead to its formation. Public space can be in many cases a form of barrier or wall. The Viennese architect Camillo Sitte noted the tendency towards large size in nineteenth- century urban public spaces, and the curious new fears which they appeared to provoke in some of the people who passed through them: the terror or panic some would feel in public places he termed 'agoraphobia', literally the 'fear of the *agora*', an idea much investigated by Sitte's contemporary, Freud, later on (Vidler 2000). It's hard to maintain the conviction, after reading Freud, that public space is an unalloyed good. For Freud – whose patients were universally well-heeled members of the Viennese bourgeoisie, and who ought to have been well adjusted to spaces built essentially in their name – public space was more often than not terrifying, city streets and squares framing for the great analyst as well as his patients feelings of fear, uncanny, or terror (for example, Freud 1985: 359). For a more contemporary illustration of the same problem, consider Brasília. If nothing else, this is a city that exalts public space, elevating it above everything else. Most of the area of the planned city is public parkland in which anyone may wander at will; residential buildings, offices and local shops, and government buildings are all set in a giant public park, open to all; on special occasions it's full of people. But according to a local architect, Fred de Holanda, it's widely appreciated by middle-class residents, while resented by poorer ones (Holanda 2000: 32). For the wealthy, the connotations of parkland are appreciated; it's precisely its emptiness and wildness that are appreciated as they speed through by car. They also appreciate the security it represents, a de facto wall separating the poor fringes of the city from the wealthy centre. For the poor themselves, the public space is a menace, a dangerous void that must be traversed on foot.

For the contemporary advocates of public space, the biggest problem of all, however, is the precise *locus* of community. By this I mean the imagined place of community: *where* it is supposed to exist. There is widespread nostalgia for a world in which all living functions could be contained in one geographical place. There are still parts of the world in which this place-based model of community is still effective, even parts of the developed world. But for highly urbanised economies such as Britain's, with marked mobility of labour, dense networks of transport, and a high degree of consumer choice, such a model rarely makes much sense. Although often advocated, the place-based model of community has long been no more than a fantasy. As the sociologist Melvin Webber argued as long ago as 1964 in the essay 'The nonplace urban realm', place in the developed world has long been supplanted by space (or more accurately, *spaces*). Most professional workers, he argued, had multiple relationships during the working day, only some of which (mediating office disputes, parental roles in the home) were dependent on geographical place. The majority of his or her relationships were conducted at great and variable distances, using communications technologies. Such relationships – however geographically distant – were as significant as anything proximate. Hence his key notion of 'community without propinquity', in other words the claim that meaningful communities might form in the absence of geographical proximity, by phone, or mail, or other means (Webber 1964: 118).

For Webber, communication networks were therefore key. His thinking strongly informed the character of the English new town, Milton Keynes, constructed from 1967. Here was a town whose form was polycentric from the start. It had a nominal centre, but of negligible importance by comparison with traditional town centres. It nevertheless had an excellent network of highways, sublimating mobility. The plan was for a civilised, urbane, connected place, in which the production of a sense of civic identity was, crucially, unconnected with the gathering of all of that community in one geographical place.

Webber was writing long before the advent of the internet, but his imagination of society in terms of information networks rather than geographical places now seems remarkably prescient. The development of social networking websites such as MySpace and Second Life during the past five years has produced extraordinary changes to the way that socialisation might happen in the developed world. We are now much more used to the idea that social life might have – but does not necessarily need – a manifestation in the physical world. The use of cell phones, for example, has direct relations with physical places, yet their use does not suppose that public physical space is any longer especially privileged. It may increase the use of certain physical spaces by making it easier to meet in them. But it may also mean that the physical inhabitants of these places are in some senses *not* there, as they are communicating with people elsewhere. This is not, and should not be, a cause for regret. It merely indicates how the use and understanding of space has changed.

Good examples of the way public space has changed through the use of modern technologies can be found all over the developed world, but particularly in newer settlements. Consider for a moment Atlanta, one of the largest and fastest growing urban areas in the United States, but also one of its least densely populated – it has barely a third of the density of Los Angeles, itself a city spread with unusual thinness. On the northern outskirts of Atlanta, some 20 miles from downtown, is a small, mostly middle-class city, Roswell, which I have often visited over the past ten years. I have got to know it quite well. Aside from a handful of nineteenth-century buildings defining a tiny historic core, this is a centreless, ex-urban sprawl of some 88,000, spread thinly over 42 square miles (see www.ci.roswell.ga.us). With no central gathering places in a European sense, no street life, and a landscape dominated by highways and gated suburbs, Roswell is the most unpromising material for a sense of community. And yet – judging from my own limited experience – its residents are as civic-minded as you could find anywhere. They vote assiduously in local elections, they organise a bewildering range of activities for their children, they take schooling (and the governance of schools) very seriously, they attend church. They operate as any middle-class city in the developed world does, but they don't for the most part produce physical expressions of community life. I find it hard to argue that this place is any more or less community-minded than Greenwich Village or Siena or Notting Hill. In some ways it is a better expression of community, if one traditional index of community life – churchgoing – is elevated.

How do we conclude? Surprisingly, perhaps, given the argument I have just made. I like public space, and would argue for more of it, simply because it is *interesting*. If you don't have it, you miss out on something. You miss out on a range of spatial experiences that you don't otherwise have. It's an education to learn to be in public spaces, as many parts of the world place great store by public space as much as there are parts of the world that do not. It's good to know what it is to be like in a place – like Brasília – where the public realm makes you feel very small. Equally, it's good to experience the licensed disorder of a Spanish street during a *fiesta*. And it is good to know something of the grand formality of nineteenth-century public spaces of Milan or Paris, and the civilised, moderate behaviour these spaces are supposed to produce. But we should separate our desire for public space from our desire for community: they are only loosely connected, if at all. Instead, let's make arguments for public space on different, and firmer, grounds.

REFERENCES

Bohigas, O. (1999) 'Ten points for an urban methodology', *Architectural Review*, 206, 1231, September, pp. 88–91.

Freud, S. (1985) *The Penguin Freud Library Vol. 14: Art and Literature*, London, Penguin Books.

Greater London Authority (2002) 'Making space for Londoners', www.london.gov.uk/mayor/auu/docs/making_space.pdf (accessed 26 June 2008)

Holanda, F. de (2000) 'Brasília beyond ideology', *Docomomo Journal*, 23, August, pp. 28–34.

Mace, R. (1976) *Trafalgar Square, Emblem of Empire*, London, Lawrence and Wishart.

Rogers, R. (1997) *Cities for a Small Planet*, London, Faber and Faber.

Rykwert, J. (2000) *The Seduction of Place*, London, Weidenfeld and Nicholson.

Sennett, R. (1994) *The Body and the City in Western Civilization*, New York and London, Norton.

Vidler, A. (2000) *Warped Space: Art, Architecture and Anxiety in Modern Culture*, Cambridge (Mass.) and London, MIT Press.

Webber, M. (1964) *Explorations into Urban Structure*, Philadelphia, University of Pennsylvania Press.

Williams, R.J. (2004) *The Anxious City: English Urbanism at the End of the Twentieth Century*, London, Routledge.

Part II

Constructing Communities

4

New New Urbanism

Austin Williams

Twenty years ago, in his BBC *Omnibus* television essay, Prince Charles called for new communities to be developed that would engender within them 'a sense of pride' (*Omnibus* 1988). In that influential programme and subsequent book, *A Vision of Britain*, he suggested that community values could be built into the very fabric of architecture and advocated that everyone ought to contribute to the planning and organisation of such an urbanism. That idea became realised in Poundbury, a new town development (or 'urban village' as Charles prefers to call it) on 400 acres of his own Duchy of Cornwall land.

While Charles's social idyll has been much parodied for its pretentious traditionalism and its faux-authenticity, this chapter argues that the underlying message – his paternalistic assertion that architects should intervene to remedy the fragmentation of what is now called 'social capital' – has been taken on board by most of the architectural community in the intervening period. Writing about the 1980s, one author confirms that, at that time, these issues reflected and generated very real 'tensions in architecture' (Larkham 1996: 21) but now, even though we may still scoff at Prince Charles's 'Ten

Principles of (Traditional) Design' (Prince of Wales 1989), they actually capture uncontentious contemporary urban anxieties. Just taking a few of his Ten Principles at random shows how mainstream this once ridiculed, and often ignored, position of New Urbanism has become. His feudal insistence that we 'respect the land' is no longer a statement of the farm-owning gentry but a modern environmental orthodoxy; his technophobic rejection of streetlamps for their 'alien sodium glow' nowadays manifests itself in chattering-class debates about 'light pollution'; and his chauffeur-driven hopes that communities will not be 'entirely sacrificed to the car' chimes with the current mantra of sustainable transport.

Architectural young fogey Ptolemy Dean recently voted the little town of Heighington in County Durham as Britain's 'perfect village' because of its 'strong sense of community' (*Northern Echo* 2006) centred on the village green. Both he and Prince Charles, like others in favour of New Urbanism (or neo-traditionalism), clearly have a vicarage tea party and summer fete version of community in mind. Indeed Poundbury is Prince Charles's way of reliving community relations from a long lost period of deference. However, 'Jam and Jerusalem' and bygone tales of communal virtue are not merely the preserve of New Urbanists. Nowadays, everyone it seems wants to wallow in the alleged certainties of the past, principally as a way of evading the present.

Notwithstanding many contemporary architects' wholesale rejection of Poundbury's amalgam of stylised tweeness, there is no longer any meaningful counter-position to the single-minded desire to engineer healthy community relations using 'socially responsible principles' (Torma 1998/1999). New Urbanism often ends up as a comic-book representation of community-friendly design; but in the more mainstream architectural firmament, architectural devices for community-building are no less contrived, with the Commission for Architecture and the Built Environment (CABE) advocating that architects be engaged in 'designing communities' ensuring that architects need to prevent a 'downward spiral' into anti-social behaviour (CABE 2003: 2). Practically all architecture now attempts to force social solidarity into existence and, by definition, condemns those who do not conform.

The BBC's ex-business commentator Jeff Randall rants that today's 'fouling of our streets, parks and countryside reflects a strain of moral degeneracy that blights a civilised society' (Randall 2007). But such a criticism is more likely to represent his own subjective moral collapse – rather than any objective measure of society's moral degradation. America's *Time* magazine, for example, records that 'Britons are frightened of their own young' (Mayer 2008).

As such, Randall *et al.* wish themselves transported back to a fictitious period of harmony of the past, while calling for authoritarian redress in the here and now. It is a complaint one hears increasingly these days, but as social commentator Stuart Waiton argues elsewhere in this book, the real problem – or moral collapse – is the corrosion of adult character such that it believes itself to be insufficiently robust to confront children's errant behaviour, preferring instead to avoid confrontation. UK journalist Madeleine Bunting sees adults 'withdraw[ing] into bunkers of the like-minded, vacating the territory of solidarity and common purpose' (Bunting 2008). What she fails to grasp is that the bunker mentality *is* the new common territory. Public space – the space occupied by the public – is now regularly seen as a threatening rather than a socialising arena.

The government's national audit of urban performance, 'State of the English Cities', explicitly defines the urban experience through the prism of 'nuisance' and suggests 'an intuitive hierarchy of priorities for citizens' (Parkinson *et al.* 2006: 167). Under this schema, the absence of 'teenagers hanging around' is now apparently one of the key signifiers of a good place to live. Actually, it could be argued – but seldom is – that the *presence* of teenagers hanging around signifies a certain intergenerational urban liveliness that comes from the visibility of youth. But in today's version of the ideal community, children should, it seems, be neither seen nor heard.

For all the talk at the beginning of the new millennium of urban regeneration bringing with it a thriving café culture, boulevards and loft apartments, these gains were always premised on the misanthropic belief that certain sections of society would undermine that pristine urban vision. As such, it became an article of faith that in order for it to be a success, those problems would have to be eradicated or admonished. So the ground rules for the so-called *urban renaissance* were laid out by the previous deputy prime minister John Prescott who said that: 'Tackling failure, such as litter, graffiti, fly-tipping, abandoned cars, dog fouling, the loss of play areas or footpaths, for many people is the top public service priority' (Prescott 2002), by which he meant that if people cannot look after their own areas, what would be the point of providing decent infrastructure and urban investment plans? As newsreader-turned-commentator Jeremy Paxman notes, 'If they see clean and tidy, they act clean and tidy. If they see squalor, they act squalid' (Paxman 2007). Such is the contemptuous starting point for the new urban discourse. Tellingly, the Commission for Architecture and the Built

Environment, a body that describes itself as an improver 'in people's quality of life through good design' (CABE 2007), was actually brought into statutory existence under the rules of the 'Clean Neighbourhoods and Environment Act 2005' (Stationary Office 2005) (appearing in the Act after the clauses on 'stray dogs' and before the clauses on 'abandoned shopping trolleys').

The government's observation that 'degraded public spaces are not a sign of a vibrant community' (DCLG 2002) may or may not be true, but has been interpreted of late as the need for people to be seen to exalt public spaces as a precursor to the aforementioned 'vibrant community' coming into existence.

Therefore, to prove that a community is worthy of support, it has to constantly monitor its actions, and those who don't match up to the requirements will be cited as the villains of the piece. This approach contains the essence of the Victorian concept of the deserving and undeserving poor. Why spend on infrastructure, the argument goes, if the 'underlying problems' (Home Office 2008) of anti-social behaviour go unresolved? Inevitably, as a result of this mindset, urban solutions begin to focus solely on solving local problems with small-scale solutions. By definition, gone are the radical, humanist architectural ideals and ambitious political masterplans. Worse still, we are left with the acceptance of the mantra that good community behaviour will warrant improved infrastructure. Urban progress and social development in the UK have not been premised on such a patrician view of the populace since the Dark Ages. But by accepting this level of political condescension, urbanism becomes a never-ending process of parochial clean-up campaigns where the putative higher ideals are always just out of reach and the objective becomes simply an insidious aim of 'promoting positive behaviour' (Home Office 2008: p. 25) and 'encouraging localism'.

Even though it is true that people 'participating in their local areas ... can make a difference' (Blackmore 2006) the flip-side of the argument – and the one that has been fully adopted by pragmatic architectural arbiters – suggests that those *not* participating are the problem. Mainstream architecture is complicit in this fearful interpretation of the world outside: a world in need of corrective, behavioural treatment. The way that it is presented today suggests that you need only to solve the problem of anti-social behaviour through design and you will be on the way to achieving social harmony. Actually, not only is this a *non sequitur* but it also reveals an instrumental approach which poisons the creative ambitions allegedly contained within architecture.

This deterministic agenda argues that building community relations will generate civic pride and thence a thriving economy. Actually, throughout history, the reverse has generally been found to be true: towns built monuments as an expression of their wealth and productive dynamism giving rise to a certain civic pride, not the other way around. The Institute for Public Policy Research (IPPR) recently advocated an ahistorical approach to creating 'civic' architecture (by definition, an artificial civic architecture) in order that community engagement could be stimulated. By building a town hall, it suggested, we could recreate the civic engagement of the 1930s when town halls were focal points of the local political landscape. The fact that it failed is unsurprising; the fact that it was roundly supported is the bigger problem.

The instrumental approach to 'making community' figures highly in the Charter for the New Urbanism. But across all architectural styles, the one question that seems no longer to be worth asking is: is it possible, or desirable, to make communities? Practically all architects and urbanists recognise that community values are in decline and believe that they have a moral and social responsibility to reinstate them. Remarkably, for a key component of all enlightened architectural discourse it is interesting that no one has the first idea what community really means let alone how it is to be achieved. (As an aside, even 'urbanism' has now become a definitional disaster area: the *Dictionary of Urbanism* helpfully defining it as 'an indefinable quality' (Cowan 2005: 431).) It is symptomatic of their collapse of nerve and acceptance of governmental edicts that practitioners fail to ask, and rush headlong into behavioural change policies that twenty years ago would have been unthinkably intrusive.

Hardly any discussion is being had on whether contemporary attempts to engineer uniformity of behaviour are helpful. And certainly no architect is asking whether it is any of their business to indulge official policy initiatives in such a crass manner. As a result of the ineptitude of this overall approach, few question why these artificial community strategies actually give rise to uncertainty, blame, tension and a blasé attitude to social control. Many simply assume that they haven't been interventionist enough! With or without debate, the truth is that the intervention of contemporary community-generating architecture fundamentally undermines the very notion of genuine community that it seeks to engender. Many of us recognised it when Disney tried it in his sterile New Urban development at Celebration in Florida, but just because many modern architects do it *sans* picket fencing, are we really that oblivious to the identical coercion inherent in their designs?

New Urbanists have been arguing about community values for decades when few would listen. They would dominate the discussion were it not for the fact that the New Urbanist movement contains images and allegiances that many self-respecting modern architects cannot be seen to accept (for example, its belief that the defining feature of a metropolis is its topographical constraints). However, the appearance of the rejection of New Urbanism masks the fact that very many contemporary architects have no other intellectual framework to offer and so they unthinkingly spout modern interpretations of New Urbanist community ambitions. The platitudes don't end there. The UK Department for Communities and Local Government defines a 'sustainable community' as one in which 'the community is active, inclusive and safe, well run, environmentally sensitive, well designed and built, well connected, thriving, well served and fair for everyone' (DCLG 2005). It's all very general, but the collective mainstream architectural community cannot be seen to be falling back on unreconstructed New Urbanism and so this type of platitude – substituting 'sustainable communities' for 'New Urban communities' – is what masquerades as urban 'theory'. What, in the past, might have resulted in architects tearing themselves on the horns of this ideological dilemma, has led to nothing other than an uncritical transition from hi-tech or such-like to 'traditional' values.

It is precisely because of the lack of intellectual and critical rigour in this debate that even though there is no architectural existential crisis, there is uncertainty about what it all really means. The fact that no one really knows is precisely the reason why this situation ends up more about process than product, but that doesn't stop the community industry from pretending to have a strategy. As such, the Academy for Sustainable Communities (ASC) was set up to counter the 'significant shortage of qualified professionals with the necessary skills' to deliver sustainable communities (ASC 2007: 3).

In his attempt strenuously to refute the idea that community should be imposed from above, Prince Charles insisted that engagement has to be built from below ... but with the help, direction and authority from community activists centrally trained, managed and maintained from on high. While it is clearly not hypocritical for an unelected head of state to advocate this type of sham community engagement, the fact that such top-down grassroots advocacy is not seen as a contradiction in terms, and has now entered the mainstream, is worrying. David Miliband MP, for instance, noted that third party agents can reach communities 'in ways that we in the statutory sector often talk about and fail to do' (Miliband 2005). So a government minister is advocating yet more unelected tiers of community liaison support because he feels unable to represent them directly. It's one thing having an education minister who cannot recall the colours of the rainbow (Borland 2008), but a communities minister who finds himself unable to engage with communities makes a bit of a mockery of the electoral process.

Miliband's aspiration for developing a sense of 'belonging and pride in their community' now comes with a 'multi-agency approach' of overseers (or 'external facilitators' (DCLG 2007)) to ensure that we create the right sort of community. This insidious interventionist rubric has become the essence of mainstream political urbanism for our times and is fundamentally opposed to a society of free agents. So much so that community strategists now warn of the dangers of 'competing interests' (Harkins 2005), i.e. other people's views; and worry that left to their own devices, 'self-appointed voice gatekeepers' (McNulty 2006: 37) will dominate. The idea that ordinary people, in actual communities, will start making demands is terrifying to the advocates of new New Urban communities. To that end, there is an Institute of Community Cohesion set up to research, monitor and document new ways of engineering cohesion; and Urban Forum, a leading umbrella organisation for community regeneration, which demands a 'designated Minister for cohesion' (Urban Forum 2007).

Without irony, anti-democratic imposition can now be presented as a necessary means of preserving democracy, and community can only be trusted if it first learns to behave responsibly. Whereas, twenty years ago, political debate regularly exposed the lack of citizens' rights in the British republic, today we are encouraged to wallow in our subject status. Where once we argued for universal supply of decent housing for all in a national framework, nowadays our subjugation is to a suspicious localised community ethos.

Fortunately, there are still some architectural commentators who find change more appealing than stasis. Stephen Bayley, writing on the tenth anniversary of Prince Charles's plasticised vision of Britain at Poundbury, said that 'English life is contaminated by the unhealthy residues of the past' (Bayley 2003). Le Corbusier drew more strident conclusions: 'Our world,' he wrote nearly 80 years ago, 'like a charnel-house, is strewn with the detritus of old dead epochs. The great task incumbent on us is that of making a proper environment for our existence, and clearing away from our cities the dead bones that putrefy in them. We must construct cities for to-day' (Le Corbusier 1971). Hyperbole aside, the essence of the modernist project of making a future that doesn't replicate the past, and certainly doesn't consciously *seek* to replicate the past, is sadly missing in architectural discourse.

But you don't need to be a modernist to appreciate the historic ambition for flux. Even romantic, morally driven Victorian architect Augustus Pugin argued that instead of copying the past, architects should incorporate 'any modern invention' that might lend itself to 'comfort, cleanline or durability' (Hill 2007).

The problem is that there are no longer any critical architectural voices in this one-sided dialogue. Those who position themselves as radical or challenging are still fully complicit in the community agenda that advocates the need to change people's behaviour in a completely instrumental way. In the 1980s, the oft-heard criticism was that public space was being privatised; now private space is being made public and there is not one significant voice raised in condemnation. We are no longer meant to inhabit public space as private individuals, but instead are charged with acting as publicly accountable persons at all times; we are expected to behave in a way that is publicly acceptable or risk having one's collar felt. No chewing, no spitting, no running, no smoking, no acting suspiciously, and no assuming that your erstwhile innocuous actions cannot be met with moral opprobrium, challenged and stopped. Architectural commentators and policy wonks are content to demand that civic space, urban realm and architectural design engender the 'correct', socially responsible response. American architectural educationalists now cite the putative benefits of 'sustainable design's emphasis on logical principles and communal values' and chastise architects for their selfish belief that 'personal expression rules' (Gould and Hosey 2006: 22).

Exactly twenty years ago, Prince Charles asked, 'Whatever happened to architects' and designers' humility?' (Prince of Wales 1989). Fortunately, architects have always tended to be an arrogant breed, trying to make a mark on the world through the conscious intervention of their intellects and actions. Unfortunately, in the twenty years since he posed the question, the belief in unfettered urbanism has taken a battering and architectural humility is making a comeback. Given its reactionary origins, it isn't surprising that New Urbanism has taken on the mantle of community patronage; what is less digestible is the creeping notion that everyone else has adopted the same position.

REFERENCES

Architecture Network (2005) 'Arts Council England appoints Chris Murray', press release, 22 December

ASC (2007) 'Mind the skills gap: the skills we need for sustainable communities – summary report', Academy for Sustainable Communities

Bayley, S. (2003) 'A cultural cul-de-sac', *Independent On Sunday*, 21 July

Blackmore, A. (2006) Head of Policy, National Council for Voluntary Organisations, press statement, '"Double devolution" moves closer to realisation with the Lyons review, says NCVO', Local Government Association, 9 August

Borland, S. (2008) 'Ed Balls red-faced after "Singing a Rainbow"', *Daily Telegraph*, 11 January

Bunting, M. (2008) 'From buses to blogs, a pathological individualism is poisoning public life', *Guardian*, 28 January

CABE (2003) 'Building sustainable communities: actions for housing market renewal', Commission for Architecture and the Built Environment, June

CABE (2004) 'Policy note preventing anti-social behaviour in public spaces', Commission for Architecture and the Built Environment, November

CABE (2007) 'Who we are. What we do. Why it matters: an introduction to CABE', Commission for Architecture in the Built Environment, 1 March

Cowan, R. (2005) *The Dictionary of Urbanism*, London, Streetwise Press

DCLG (2002) 'Living places: cleaner, safer, greener', Department for Communities and Local Government, p. 12

DCLG (2005) 'Local strategic partnerships: shaping their future', Department for Communities and Local Government

DCLG (2007) Report by the Comptroller and Auditor General, HC 20 Session 2007–2008, Department for Communities and Local Government, 'Housing market renewal', National Audit Office, 9 November, p. 9

Gould, K. and Hosey, L. (2006) *Ecological Literacy in Architecture Education: 2006 Report and Proposal*, AIA Committee on the Environment

Harkins, E. (2005) 'Leadership in the community: a SURF summary paper', Networking Initiatives, Scottish Urban Regeneration Forum

Hill, R. (2007) *God's Architect, Pugin & the Building of Romantic Britain*, London, Allen Lane

Home Office (2008) Respect Agenda, www.respect.gov.uk (accessed 3 January 2008)

Larkham, P. (1996) *Conservation and the City*, London, Routledge

Le Corbusier (1971) *The City of Tomorrow and its Planning*, London, The Architectural Press

Mayer, C. (2008) 'Britain's mean streets', *Time*, 26 May

McNulty, D. (2006) 'Shaping the future with a nod to the past and present', in John Benington, Lucy de Groot and Jane Foot (eds), *Lest We Forget: Democracy, Neighbourhoods and Government*, London, Solace Imprint Foundation, November

Miliband, D. (2005) 'Speech by the Rt Hon David Miliband MP to the Core Cities Group; civic pride for the modern age', Core Cities Group, 20 May

Northern Echo (2006) BBC 4's 'Perfect village' cited in 'Village is the most perfect in Britain', 9 September

Omnibus (1988) Prince Charles, 'A vision of Britain', BBC 1, 28 October

Parkinson, M. *et al.* (2006) *State of the English Cities: A Research Study*, Office of the Deputy Prime Minister, March, Volume 1, p. 167

Paxman, J. (2007) 'Green and pleasant land?' *Guardian*, 6 March

Prescott, J. (2002) 'Living places: cleaner, safer, greener', Office of the Deputy Prime Minister, Ministerial Foreword, October

Prince of Wales (1989) 'Prince of Wales' ten principles of (traditional) design', *A Vision of Britain: A Personal View of Architecture*, Doubleday

Randall, J. (2007) 'Louts are trashing our green and pleasant land', *Daily Telegraph*, 18 May

Stationary Office (2005) 'Clean Neighbourhoods and Environment Act 2005', Chapter 16, Part 8, Clause 87

Torma, C. (Fall 1998/Winter 1999) 'Prince Charles builds a new town', *The Commissioner*, American Planning Association

Urban Forum (2007) 'The empowerment game, first results', The Empowerment Game – Chance or Community Chest? Urban Forum Annual Conference, 3–4 December, www.urbanforum.org.uk (accessed 5 May 2008)

5
Density Versus Sprawl

Karl Sharro

Two-thirds of people in Britain live in a suburban context of one form or another. When questioned about their ideal home, the majority of people express a preference for a detached or semi-detached house. Evidence suggests that suburbs, low-density housing in planning jargon, are very desirable. Regardless of their obvious popularity, there have been intensifying attacks on suburbs among politicians, academics, architects and media pundits in the last few years. Among professionals, this is known as the density versus sprawl debate. In reality, there is very little debate going on. Planning policies are becoming more anti-suburban, and the few commentators who have come to the defence of suburbs have been largely dismissed. Part of their failure is that they have treated this as a technical discussion when in fact it is a deeply political one. Like so many other aspects of our lives, the collusion between officialdom and self-appointed reformers propagates the claim that they know what is best for us, including where and how we should live. There is no meaningful outcome for a density versus sprawl debate, people should have the choice. However, there is an important defence to be made of the democratisation of housing that suburbs represent.

In keeping with this book's mission of exploring the future of community this chapter will mainly address the claims that suburban developments are intrinsically anti-social and that they have contributed to the weakening of communal and social bonds. To be sure, that is not the only claim made against suburbs; they are blamed for causing obesity and health problems because they encourage dependency on cars and discourage walking and cycling. Suburban developments are accused of having a severe environmental impact because they consume land and resources. And in films such as *Blue Velvet* (1986) and *American Beauty* (1999) they are depicted as morally corrupt landscapes where people's tendencies for depravity can flourish. The one aspect in common to all these critiques is that of loss of control: of the city, of the countryside, of community and of the body. Those critics chose to interpret the experience of modernity in the twentieth century as that of a runaway train, of things getting out of hand and human beings being swamped by trends that are not under their control. In as much as there is a commonality to these critiques, the theme of loss of control is quite instrumental towards understanding why suburbia today is derided by the decision makers and favoured by citizens.

The theme of loss of control regularly manifests itself in discussions about urbanism and the experience of modernity in general. Richard Rogers, the architect and chairman of the Urban Task Force, is one of the most vocal and influential critics of suburbia. When he delivered his Megacities lecture in 2001, he opened with a direct attack on America, claiming that it has the worst sustainability record in the western world as well as the worst record of riots. Combining the images of environmental catastrophe and social breakdown, he attributed those 'failures' to America's refusal to plan cities. Rogers blatantly ignores the long American tradition of rational city planning and ambitious infrastructure projects and equates the American experience in urbanism with the proliferation of suburbs. To his mind, and indeed to many others, America's refusal to contain the expansion of suburbia contributed to the loss of control over society and the environment.

Rogers's understanding of planning is representative of a contemporary aversion to development. To him, planning is not about the universal provision of services and infrastructure that allows a modern society to develop but about the strict control and regulation of the process of development. It is worth noting that Rogers titled his lecture 'The fragmented city and the role of the architect'. This choice of words immediately problematises the density question by precluding any objective discussion on the merits of low-density development. The frequent use of the term 'sprawl' reinforces this bias, implying a loss of control over the physical shape of the city. Furthermore, Rogers's title implies an ailing urban form that is in need of remedial intervention, from the architect who can piece the city back together. But how?

Rogers's prescriptive solution relies strongly on the concept of design. In the Urban Task Force final report, *Towards an Urban Renaissance* (1999), 'achieving design excellence' was one of the main recommendations towards achieving that reversal in the fortunes of cities. On the surface, this appears to be articulating the desire for better quality in the built environment. On closer examination, those recommendations reveal a strong authoritarian impulse that equates design excellence with the authors' aesthetic preferences and cultural assumptions. Design is discussed as a tool for enabling staged and scripted encounters, instead of a tool for innovation in housing and urban forms.

This discussion of the role of design highlights the resurgence of environmental determinism. The popularity of this concept reveals why suburbs are often blamed for the decline of community, but it also legitimises intrusive and authoritarian measures in the name of reform. In the decade since the Urban Task Force report was published, utilising design to actively condition the behaviour of individuals has become increasingly acceptable. We regularly hear from criminologists about the benefits of 'designing out crime', and recently there were suggestions that towns and cities need to be radically redesigned to tackle the obesity epidemic (Henderson 2008). In the same spirit, architects and designers now regularly talk about how cities can be designed to allow users, or force them rather, to be more sociable. Not long ago, such suggestions of explicit official intervention in our daily life would have brought images of Orwellian horror to mind. Today, we seem more willing to tolerate this intrusiveness, if not welcome it.

It is against this background that we need to place the discussion about density and community today. Socialisation is promoted as a matter for experts and officials to orchestrate, rather than something we willingly take part in. Richard Rogers is explicit in blaming suburbia for the demise of community: 'At what point does the countryside become town? If I have a problem it's with suburban sprawl – which is neither one thing nor another because it has no community' (Jackson and Rogers 2001). This view is echoed by many, in fact it has become something of an orthodoxy. Yet the assumption on which it is based goes unexamined:

that being part of a community is dictated by circumstances rather than by the willingness of individuals to seek each other's company.

Part of the confusion behind these assumptions is the common misunderstanding of the concepts of community and society. Community emphasises the notion of the familiar and implies a narrower geography limited to the scale of a neighbourhood. Society, on the other hand, reflects an organisation through which strangers can have meaningful encounters, and even for them to have common causes without the benefit of familiarity. That requires a much more complex form of social organisation in which free socialisation could flourish, and that is precisely what the metropolitan experience represents. That architects and officials prefer to express their ideas on socialisation in reference to neighbourhoods and villages is indicative of their limited understanding of what makes a civilised society.

Indeed, that limitation extends to their understanding of the city, which is often described in cosy and parochial language. 'In terms of the anatomy of the city, the city is a series of villages and towns put together. The neighbourhood community is the beginning, the doorstep if you like' (Jackson and Rogers 2001). Only two years before Rogers delivered his lecture, Deyan Sudjic critiqued in his Megacities lecture this romantic notion of communities:

Urban communities are more symbolic expressions than physical realities. The ideal urban community is presented as if urban families occupied a dynastic homestead for life, which they would pass on to their children and their children's children. It presupposes a Mediterranean fishing village social organisation with land held in common, and a strongly hierarchical social structure in which elders are natural leaders, deferred to by their younger contemporaries. Even

> if the kind of stability on which a community of that kind depends did
> exist, it is by no means clear that it would present a desirable option
> for most city dwellers. (Sudjic 1999)

Sudjic also made the point that the nature of cities changes over time:

> A city of 40 million has no historic parallel. When Rome had one
> million residents, the whole of Europe was less than 40 million people.
> Now a single city can reach that size. These are urban organisms whose
> scale, geography, form and institutions makes [sic] them entirely new
> in the history of human experience. And we need to find new ways of
> living in such places, and new techniques of analysis to understand
> them. (Sudjic 1999)

Suffice it to say that a city such as London today is not the same as Florence during the Renaissance or medieval Paris. Yet this is precisely the way in which the prevailing *urbanistas* choose to understand community life in the city today: through reference to medieval market places and town squares:

> My lecture today is about the compact city – if you look at a typical
> example of a medieval lay-out, you can see that in essence the basic
> language of urban landscape has not altered so drastically – the central
> square, the church, the town hall, the market space, the network of
> roads – a highly legible, compact, mixed use organism of live, work
> and leisure – where people can easily connect. (Rogers 2001)

And therein lies the problem. In attempting to understand the nature of community life in the city today by using outdated models from the past, sociologists and architects are showing a limited grasp of the nature of the contemporary city. This is not simply an oversight or the result of intellectual laziness, but is indicative of a deeper cultural discontent with the process of change. I mentioned earlier how loss of control forms the conceptual background for the anxiety towards suburbia and what it represents. Against the backdrop of the prevailing sentiment that humanity appears to have transgressed its natural limitations, it becomes easier to understand the accompanying sense of loss of control.

The exact type of change that cities have undergone remains difficult to understand. Although nowadays it seems that cities are being discussed extensively, it is quite evident that much more effort goes into dealing with the scale of cities than goes into understanding their nature. The city has become the statistical artefact *par excellence*, as 2007's 'Global Cities' exhibition at the Tate Modern illustrated. Yet behind this glut of data and statistics there seems to be little by way of a serious analysis of the social form of the contemporary metropolis. Time and time again, commentators keep revisiting the same exhausted concepts: neighbourhood, street, square, community. When it comes to the contemporary dispersed megacities, Los Angeles, London, Mexico City, these concepts are ill-fitting, leading those commentators to condemn rather than understand these emerging urban forms. The artificial distinction that is made between the suburbs and the city only serves to compound this problem. Rather than the neat categories that this distinction implies, the reality is that of interconnected settlements which vary in density but function as part of much larger metropolitan areas. Most of these have surpassed the limits of the political and administrative areas that used to define them.

Yet this artificial distinction continues to be the background for the density–sprawl debate, further complicating what is already a convoluted discussion. For starters, this debate appears to be entirely one-sided. Unlike the heated architectural debates of the past when there were clearly defined schools of thought battling it out in public (think modernists versus historicists), this discussion is characterised by the clamour of architects and *urbanistas* met by an almost complete silence. It appears that no one wants to take credit for suburbia in its current form; those of us who wish to live there do so and are not necessarily bothered by the hectoring of architects and planners. Perhaps this is because suburbia as we know it today is an orphan: a unique phenomenon in housing that was brought into being almost entirely by circumstances rather than conscious will.

Of course one could point to a certain commonality or lineage between Ebenezer Howard's Garden City or the post-war New Towns and contemporary suburbia, but that would miss the point. Both the Garden City and the New Towns were conceived as self-sufficient entities that envisioned people living and working in the same town. Suburbia today relies on the great mobility afforded by private cars and the extensive road networks that support them. In that sense, we cannot claim that suburban developments are merely accidental; they require a significant investment in infrastructure and some accommodation in planning regulations to allow access to land. In other words, they must rely on political will. The booms in suburban growth represented a democratisation of the development process that allowed millions of people to have access to better housing. That form of mass affluence is today under attack in the name of reform.

The political attitude towards suburban developments in Britain fluctuated throughout the twentieth century. The great wave of suburban developments in between the two wars was replaced directly after the Second World War with the restrictive policies that nationalised building rights and established the green belts to protect the countryside from development. The arguments that paved the way for those policies are very similar to the anti-sprawl arguments that we hear today, disproving to some extent the claim that we are facing a unique problem. In the late 1960s the great enthusiasm for motorway construction allowed the expansion of suburban developments, which also found favour in the 1980s with Margaret Thatcher's vision of increased private property ownership. By the mid-1990s, that enthusiasm had waned and both motorway construction and house building in general had fallen to historically low levels.

Against this political backdrop, the architectural profession had maintained for the most part a significant influence on the direction of housing in Britain. That was no longer the case in the last quarter of the century: the appetite for ambitious housing projects had evaporated and modernism had generally fallen into disfavour. The belief in the wisdom of the market that the Conservatives had championed and New Labour had later full-heartedly adopted made expensive state-backed visionary-ism a thing of the past. In parallel, the increasing affluence in society led to requirements for better housing, and this time around it was delivered without fanfare and manifestos by private developers.

It is not hard then to understand the animosity that architects have towards suburbia: to most of them it represents not only a bastard typology but also a challenge to their monopoly on both good taste and vision. It is a particular source of anxiety because it represents ongoing modernity without the benefit of an accompanying narrative. Throughout the twentieth century the narrative was that of modernism: the conscious break with the old in pursuit of progress. Without a vision of the new society, innovation becomes a mere stylistic exercise, and this is precisely the predicament of architecture today. It is breathlessly chasing stylistic innovations while images of medieval squares define what it understands the good society to be.

Our attitude to modernity today largely influences the way this particular episode of anti-suburbia is playing out. Material affluence, which was once seen as a noble objective for a society to pursue, is now seen as a distraction from a well-balanced life, and we're often told that the pursuit of happiness and quality of life are more important than material wealth. In the absence of the narrative of progress, the pursuit of wealth is often seen through the prism of consumerism, and there is an influential trend in social theory that seeks to portray citizens as mindless consumers whose instincts are manipulated by the media and advertising.

With the rise of this over-simplified understanding of material development and the patronising dismissal of the masses, it has become difficult to appreciate suburbs for what they provide: comfort, room and open space. Instead, they are portrayed as the choice of selfish individuals who shun social interaction for their own comforts. In a recent interview, Richard Rogers asked rhetorically: 'Do you really want to be living in the suburbs with five cats, four dogs, a cabbage patch and five rooms?' (Rogers 2007). Rogers makes the assumption that life in suburbia is insular and mindless, but this assumption is more indicative of how the elites view the masses today rather than of what life in suburbia is like. And it is precisely this negative outlook that is nowadays shaping the density debate.

Tristram Hunt is even more damning of the suburbs that Rogers. Speaking of the inter-war boom in suburban development, he says: 'In a vast transhumance, the British made their way from the cities to the low-density, low-rise housing springing up between railway stations, along arterial roads and in vast housing estates. With it came the car and a renewed rejection of society beyond the immediate family: the most sought-after suburb was one that gave the maximum privacy – behind gates, hedges and walls – and the minimum outside distraction' (Hunt 2004).

Hunt presupposes a deeply anti-social instinct that drives the English towards suburbia and away from the city. However, conscious perhaps of the great tradition of free association that thrived in this country, he hastens to remind us that:

> there is another story of British social relations. One that emphasises not the possessive individualism of the home-owner, but the associational heritage of our towns and cities. From the gentleman's clubs of London to the Mechanics [sic] Institutes of Bolton to the Halle [sic] Orchestra, Hermann Muthesius ignored our vibrant tradition of civil society. Lectures, concerts, political rallies and civic ceremonials, at which women were welcome participants, turned Britain's cities into cultural fiefdoms. (Hunt 2004)

Hunt fails to explain how the same citizens who participated in this cultural tradition would readily abandon the city for a suburban homestead, and how once they got there the social impulse would desert them. Hunt, the vociferous anti-suburbanite, attributes this social and cultural drive to the proximity and the density of the city rather than to a human desire for social interaction. But as one commentator with far more insight into human affairs reminds us: 'To imagine that there is anything in physical proximity that is essential to community is to confuse animal warmth with civilisation, and an unfortunately deterministic view of architecture's relationship to society' (Heartfield 2006: 67).

If the reports of social decline in Britain are accurate, and I personally remain to be convinced that they are, I think we need to look for the causes elsewhere than in suburbia. What the discussion about density and community reveals is an extreme bias among commentators and decision makers against the suburbs and an aversion towards their residents. One thing is for sure: pushing people forcefully into closer proximity will not deliver the urban renaissance or revive communities, but will only strengthen the intrusive micro-management of our daily lives.

The sense of a loss of control that typifies public discourse today is not an accurate reflection of reality, but an expression of a cultural mindset. When it frames the discussion of density and suburbia it makes fetishes of both. There is no inherent moral value in either; how we choose to interpret both today is a reflection of cultural pessimism rather than objective assessment. Withdrawing from the technological and scientific achievements of the past century represents a collective failure of nerves, seeking the perverse comfort afforded by the knowledge that we have reached our limits and that we can linger safely in the status quo. Yet those perceived limits are only self-imposed limits on the imagination. It is time to challenge this downbeat attitude and re-imagine the new city and the new society. There is ample land in Britain to build the former, and it is only by resisting the intrusion of the state and the tyranny of so-called experts that we can build the latter.

REFERENCES

Heartfield, J. (2006) *Let's Build: Why We Need Five Million New Homes in the Next 10 Years*, London, Audacity

Henderson, M. (2008) 'Welcome to the town that will make you lose weight', *The Times*, 18 February

Hunt, T. (2004) 'How the English became obsessed with property', *New Statesman*, 2 February

Jackson, J. and Rogers, R. (13.6.2001) 'Mr. Town meets Mr. Country', *openDemocracy*, 16 June, www.opendemocracy.net/ecology-movements/article_434.jsp/ (accessed 16 March 2008)

Rogers, R. (2001) 'The fragmented city and the role of the architect', The Fifth Megacities lecture, 15 November, www.megacities.nl/ (accessed 1 May 2008)

Rogers, R. (2007) 'Richard Rogers', *Icon Magazine*, Issue 049, July

Sudjic, D. (19.11.1999) 'Identity in the city', The Third Megacities lecture, 19 November, www.megacities.nl/ (accessed 1 May 2008)

Urban Task Force (1999) *Towards an Urban Renaissance*, London

6
Salvation by Brick?
The Life and Death of
British Communities

Penny Lewis

Geoffrey Scott in *The Architecture of Humanism* (1914) wrote that the history of civilisation leaves in architecture its 'truest but most unconscious record' (Scott 1980: 16). Today the character of our built environment provides a reasonably accurate reflection of the nature of our economic and social life. You could say that Mumbai is dense and vibrant as an expression of the explosive productive energy of India's emerging economy; while in the UK, our built environment tells the story of a society in which there is sufficient individual wealth and collective infrastructure to allow for dispersed development. It suggests a society with a sluggish economy, which exercises its creative energy through consumption, in and outside of its urban centres.

From the Greeks onwards, cities have displayed a pattern of urban development that can be read as a physical expression of the character of public life and the value placed on privacy. Today, we are busy constructing 'public places' not as a spontaneous expression of public life, but as an expression of its opposite, an anxiety about the decline in social interaction and trust. For the most part, we don't seem to like the places that are spontaneously produced by economic and social life. Sometimes they are badly designed, but the common concern is that they are soulless. Perhaps they provide too stark an expression of the unrivalled and unmediated role of the market in our lives? We mostly shop in supermarkets, but many feel they are inauthentic and hanker after a world in which high streets were still populated by butchers and greengrocers instead of mobile phone outlets. We are habitually on the search for 'real places'.

The urban village or city neighbourhood provides a model of an ideal community and the setting for the type of urban lifestyle celebrated in Jane Jacobs' classic work *The Death and Life of the Great American Cities* (1961). Jacobs, whose contemporary appeal lies in the ideas she conveys of community, has become a major reference point for planners over the past two decades. Although rarely mentioning the C-word, her description of the informal networks and shared values in her local neighbourhood, and the 'urban ballet' or natural pattern of everyday city life, appeals to policy makers and, to some extent, public aspirations. In *Bowling Alone: The Collapse and Revival of American Community* (2000), Robert Putnam credits Jacobs with having invented the idea of 'social capital'.

Despite the fact that we live with a very different set of conditions from 1950s New York, contemporary policy makers insist on generalising from *Death and Life*. Put crudely, today Jacobs evokes the idea of streets with a mixture of people, buildings and uses that are both cosmopolitan and communal. These places have 'active frontages' occupied by small independent service providers: small shops, cafés and bars and housing that overlook the street and create an informal pattern of passive surveillance. Old buildings have been retained and new blocks are dense but not too high or too long.

Jacobs' observations, and her polemic against post-war planners, provide today's 'Jacobsites' with the material for two important ideas. The first is that social bonds and shared meanings begin life at a local level with the simple informal interactions of everyday life and that the erosion of these shared values and informal networks began with modern planning and zoning. The second is that through the design of the right kind of dense and diverse environments we can cultivate those social networks, agreed behaviour and shared values.

STREET LIFE

In the late 1950s, Greenwich Village was populated by upwardly mobile workers and bohemian types (dubbed 'slum romantics'). It was the start of the post-war boom and the process of 'unslumming' or 'gentrification' was coming into conflict with the city authority's plans for the modernising the city. Jacobs observed a set of relationships that developed from small commercial transactions but extended to form a framework for acceptable behaviour and a certain collective responsibility for the care and discipline of children. These relationships were thrown up by the market, but invested with some greater social meaning because of their repetitive and local character. In particular she described the way in which the adults working and shopping on the street would take responsibility for the disciplining, and safety, of children playing in the street.

Over time these shared experiences created a sense of belonging and social coherence. What is often neglected in this understanding of neighbourhood was that it was developing within a broader social and political context: the USA's post-war boom. It's the broader context, particularly the optimism about the possibility of social improvement, that shaped the character of the everyday relationships between people.

Jacobs was describing a certain social solidarity, which she and others sensed was being undermined. This sociological shift coincided with modernisation and suburbanisation and so in Jacobs' work the two are closely linked. Since the 1950s it has become increasingly common for pundits to link planning policy with the quality of public life in a very direct deterministic fashion. When she wrote *Death and Life* there was a growing animosity among some intellectuals towards the suburbs and the monotony of middle-class 'bedroom communities'. Suburbanites, the saying went, arrived as Democrats and left as Republicans. In *The Uses of Disorder* (1970), Richard Sennett says: 'My belief is that disorder is better than dead, predetermined planning, which restricts effective social exploration. It is better for men to be makers of historical change than for the functional design of a pre-experiential plan to be "carried out"' (Sennett 1970: 142). Mono-cultural environments, argued the critics, produced one-dimensional citizens who were ill equipped to negotiate anything other than their own familiar environment.

It's interesting that these ideas about diversity have really come of age in the past decade. Today it's part of the planners' and government mantra that new settlements dominated by a single class or ethnic group are spontaneously damaging to the broader social fabric of society. As a result, planning policy is now designed to manufacture a social mix to prevent the concentration of disadvantaged, low-income groups in given geographical areas.

At the core of Jacobs' argument is the idea that good places are founded on the street and implicit is that when modern planners abandoned the primacy of the street frontage they also jettisoned public life. She argues that the historic desire in the twentieth century to make the world ordered and organised – whether it was Le Corbusier's Ville Radieuse or Howard's Garden City – destroyed social cohesion and the idea of balanced communities.

Jacobs was not the first person to suggest that modern planning might undermine social capital. The idea that re-housing is destructive because it destroys social bonds is clearly expressed in *Family and Kinship in East London*, by Michael Young and Peter Willmott (1962, first published in the USA in 1957). The study looks at family and neighbourhood relationships in Bethnal Green and how these are affected by moves to a new development in Greenleigh, Essex. The authors found that the majority wanted to stay in the East End, but moved to get houses and gardens. The book recommended the movement of street and kinship groupings as a whole rather than in nuclear families, to 'enable the city to be rebuilt without squandering the fruits of social cohesion' (Young and Willmott 1957: 198). The report went on to say:

> Even when the town planners have set themselves to create communities anew as well as houses, they still put their faith in buildings, sometimes speaking as though all that was necessary for neighbourliness was a neighbourhood unit, and for community spirit, a community centre. If this were so, then there would be no harm in shifting people about the country, for what is lost could be

regained by skilful architecture and design. But there is surely more
to a community than that. (Young and Willmott 1957: 198)

In retrospect the critics of post-war planning have recast the
process of re-housing as one of disempowerment. In reality
the process was much more complex – and often liberating
– but despite the evidence to the contrary it has become a
commonsense belief that post-war reconstruction, and in
particular the tower blocks, are responsible for the decline
in social cohesion.

In the late 1970s, Jacobs' work generated interest in the
UK. It was a period that saw the election of Rod Hackney as
head of the Royal Institute of British Architects, a community
architect involved in the rehabilitation of terraced housing
in the North of England. As Eric Hobsbawm wrote in *The
Age of Extremes* (1994), suddenly everyone was talking up
communities at the very moment when they seemed to have
almost disappeared.

Around this time the Byker development in Newcastle was
built as a polemic against post-war re-housing. Following
extensive public consultation Ralph Erskine designed the
estate so that tenants could be relocated street by street,
into housing specifically designed to reflect the needs of
individual families and extended families. By the 1990s Byker
was experiencing all of the same problems as other large
social housing estates. It had deteriorated dramatically and
was considered an undesirable area by many tenants. The
experience suggests that the problems facing post-war social
housing were much wider than those of housing design.

During the 1980s theorists made the unimaginative leap
from Jacobs' libertarian thesis to crude determinism, best
expressed in the work of Alice Coleman, most notably her

book *Utopia on Trial* published in the UK in 1985. This was a time when the post-war optimism of Greenwich Village had been replaced by the heady mix of bravado and anxiety associated with popular capitalism. Alongside opposition to the dismantling of the welfare state there was growing concern about the decline of community. Coleman argued that certain urban forms cultivated a 'complex system of interlocking levels and circles of acquaintanceship, which gives the community a clear knowledge of its accepted mores, and hence practical guidelines for behaviour – an essential framework for stability' (Coleman 1985: 9). In 2007, for all its social problems and its exposing of Coleman's flawed thesis, Byker achieved listed status and was held up as an exemplar of good design.

SALVATION BY BRICK

The relationship between society and planning is a complex one. The outcome of architectural innovation – particularly in relation to planning and housing – depends on a whole number of economic, political and social factors. Today it has become acceptable to argue that a certain type of urban design or architecture (e.g. the tower block or council housing estates) don't work without reference to the context in which they were commissioned.

This is an issue on which Jacobs was very astute. She rejected anything that smelled of paternalism. 'The trouble with paternalists is that they want to make impossibly profound changes, and they chose impossibly superficial means for doing so' (Jacobs 1992: 271). While Jacobs pioneered the idea that short blocks were better than long ones for encouraging social interaction, she did not believe that urban forms could determine human behaviour.

In *Death and Life* she explained how local housing authorities' aspiration to create a sense of togetherness through shared facilities had eroded many tenants' sense of privacy and freedom, and forced them to withdraw from public life. 'Good shelter is a useful good in its self, as shelter. When we try to justify good shelter instead on the pretentious grounds that it will work social or family miracles, we fool ourselves. Reinhold Niebuhr has called this particular self-deception, "The doctrine of salvation by brick"' (1992: 113), warned Jacobs.

Her observations about the way in which adults in Greenwich Village spontaneously took on responsibility for socialising children demonstrated a real belief in the capacity for human self-organisation: 'The myth that playgrounds and grass and hired guards or supervisors are innately wholesome for children and that city streets, filled with ordinary people, are innately evil for children, boils down to a deep contempt for ordinary people' (1992: 82), she wrote.

Take, for example, the idea of anonymity. Jacobs describes the relationship with the local shopkeeper. It's an interesting relationship. She can trust him to look after the keys for her apartment when she is expecting a visitor from out of town. She also knows that he, unlike a shopkeeper in a rural village, will not ask who the visitor is or the purpose of their visit. He respects her privacy. There is both an element of trust and a clear sense of boundaries – for anonymity is a crucial element in a city in which people are living in such close proximity.

However, Oscar Newman's work on new housing in New York had identified anonymity as a problem. Alice Coleman built on Newman's research to argue that anonymity was undermining the stability of the neighbourhood. In *Utopia on Trial* she wrote:

> Successful city neighbourhoods ... proved to be close textured, high-density assemblages of mixed land uses, where many people lived within walking distance of many destinations and there is constant coming and going on foot along a dense network of streets. This pattern works naturally to ensure the emergence of a firm social structure. (Coleman 1985: 9)

Through Coleman and others, Jacobs' ambition – the expansion and intensification of great cities – was reworked to a much more conservative framework.

In the time since Coleman, the UK has developed highly prescriptive policies that attempt to enforce inclusion, impose diversity and design-in community. When interviewed a few years before her death, Jacobs criticised the New Urbanism movement – who are often seen as inheritors of the her mantle – arguing that they didn't understand the organic and spontaneous character of places. The approach of contemporary Jacobsites is indeed inimical to the spirit of Jacobs' writings. Social solidarity within neighbourhoods in the UK is often weak regardless of the character or the quality of the built environment. The problem of community is not susceptible to the imposed solutions of urban design.

REFERENCES

Coleman, A. (1985) *Utopia on Trial*, London, Hilary Shipman

Donaldson, S. (1969) *The Suburban Myth*, Columbia University Press

Hobsbawm, E. (1994) *The Age of Extremes*, London, Michael Joseph

Jacobs, J. (1992) *The Death and Life of the Great American Cities*, New York, Random House

Putnam, R. (2000) *Bowling Alone: The Collapse and Revival of American Community*, New York, Simon & Schuster

Scott, G. (1980) *The Architecture of Humanism*, London, Architectural Press

Sennett, R. (1970) *The Uses of Disorder: Personal Identity and City Life*, New York, Vintage

Steigerwald, B. (2001) an associate editor and columnist for the Pittsburgh Tribune Review, interviewed Jacobs for *Reason* magazine, March, www.reason.com

Young, M. and Willmott, P. (1957) *Family and Kinship in East London*, London, Pelican

Part III
Communities in Flux

7
Strictly Personal:
The Working Class
Confined to Community

Andrew Calcutt

This chapter explores the way in which the emphasis on community in the prolonged aftermath of the Second World War gave shape to a model of British society in which the working class was disarmed – politically – just as it had been militarily demobilised after the war effort. In the contemporary period, it suggests that the British elite seeks to remobilise by proxy: by talking about and talking up community it is trying to talk itself into being one. In other words, it seems that the idea of community has less to do with imagined tradition and more to do with contemporary demands for social order.

DEMOB HAPPY

In waging the Second World War, Britain was unusually expansive – it recruited anyone and everyone to the war effort (sometimes drawing the line at Jews) – but also severely over-extended. In the decade after demobilisation in 1945, British society contracted. While the British ruling class withdrew from large tracts of empire, the working class was largely evacuated from the field of politics and frequently confined to domestic quarters. Headed by Michael Young, co-author of Labour's programme for the 'khaki election' of 1945 (so-called because so many voters were still in uniform waiting to be demobilised), in the 1950s and early 1960s the Institute of Community Studies gave intellectual shape to the political demobilisation of British workers and their eventual domestication.

This is not to suggest that Young *et al.* did not have good grounds for reporting what they did, yet the grounds on which they surveyed the working class, the territory on which they chose to depict it, was mapped in such a way that the extended family appeared as both the boundary and the central social bond. This had the effect of impressing the domestic on their reconstruction of working-class life, in the same way that they gave the impression that the working class was constituted largely by its recreation in the home. This construct downplayed other, social roles arising from the creation of new value in the capitalist economy and those arising from the attempt to resolve capitalist contradiction in politics.

British workers were first enlisted to fight in the Second World War, then demobilised as it came to an end. In this process, one group of actors was recruited to play three sets of impersonal relations. As workers they were already participating in the impersonal relations of economics; as union members/Labour party supporters, they entered into the continuation of economics by other means – politics; and as recruits to the British armed forces they were signing up to the further extension of politics and economics, namely, war. In the Allied celebrations of 1945 all three sets of impersonal relations were brought cheerily together as a triangle of assumptions about the post-war period.

In and of this triangle, the ex-soldier (and his family) could expect a job in a unionised workplace; a house or flat to live in built by a Labour council; and an NHS bed to lie in if he became seriously ill. After the war, not only returning soldiers, but all working-class people who identified with the wartime ethos were effectively pegged to these coordinates and their concomitant expectations. Compared to the bloody ruptures of world war, and the violent conflicts of pre-war politics, these were the demands of a remarkably stable society. But how had the mobilisation of the majority, and the potential for instability associated with the presence of millions of workers under arms, been converted into this new nation of triangulation and stabilisation? There is no scope here to trace the historical development of this process. Instead, I shall show that this was the logical outcome of a historically specific approach to the working class on the part of the British elite, as epitomised by the influential Institute of Community Studies in its own presentation of the life and times of the post-war working class.

Interviewed towards the end of his life by historian Peter Hennessy, the Institute's founder-director, Michael Young, observed that wartime solidarity was remarkable but remarkably short-lived. He reported 'an extraordinary object lesson in the power of fraternity in the war, and when the war was over it was as though that experience could be wiped out' (Dench, Gavron and Young 2006: 7). What Young did not mention is that in their descriptions of working-class life it was he and his associates who 'wiped out' the experience of 'fraternity'. In their highly influential accounts of working-class communities, such as *Family and Kinship in East London* (Young and Willmott 1957), the impersonal relations of work, politics and wartime, and the solidarities arising from them, are noticeable by their absence.

Instead, Young and Willmott characterised working people almost entirely by their personal relations. Indeed *Family and Kinship in East London* focuses on the set of the most intimate personal relations – the family – itself stretched as far as the extended family, until the community is posited as the farthest parameter of these intimate, personal relations. Of impersonal relations there was hardly a mention. Yet it was through these relations – not personal relations – that working-class Londoners had produced and transported an empire of commodities, built the Labour party and trade union movement, and, most recently, fought fascism on behalf of British interests.

In Young and Willmott's depiction of working-class people, they were drawn into a circle of personal relations which at its widest extended to community; but this is also to say that community, as assigned to working-class people by Young *et al.*, was much narrower than the social reality which they had inhabited hitherto – the reality of world war, for example. Young's research had the effect of mounting an attack on impersonal relations. In the presentation of working-class life given by the Institute of Community Studies, the generation which blew up Berlin was embedded in Bethnal Green and acting as if it had never been further afield than Barking.

Thus in the conclusion to *Family and Kinship in East London* (the template for nearly all subsequent research by the Institute of Community Studies),[1] Young and Willmott questioned the mobilisation of the masses in a modernist housing strategy that paid little regard to community and the advantages to be had from the social cohesion it brings:

> The question for the authorities is whether they should do more than they are presently doing to meet the preference of people who would not willingly forego these advantages, rather than insisting that more thousands should migrate beyond the city. (Young and Willmott 1957: 165)

Not that Young had become wholly conservative. This was, after all, the co-author of the ever-most radical Labour party manifesto (with the possible exception of the 1983 'suicide note'). Rather, he wished to maintain social cohesion in the midst of reconstruction:

> Not everyone could, under this or any other plan, hope to stay where they are. People will have to move about within their own district, if not outside it, as the slums beyond salvage are cleared and replaced. But re-shuffling the residents could be accomplished by moving as a block the social groups, above all the wider families, to which people wish to belong. Movement of street and kinship groupings as a whole, members being transferred together to a new setting, would enable the city to be rebuilt without squandering the fruits of social cohesion. (Young and Willmott 1957: 165–6)

Young's account of social relations had the effect of reducing social cohesion to the rubble of personal relations – i.e. that which is left when impersonal relations are taken out of the picture. While impersonal relations have hardly amounted to the full-blown construction of a different kind of community – the community of communism – nonetheless, they have served as the scaffolding by which modern generations sought to raise themselves above the ground-level of interpersonal relations. But in Young's depiction of it, working-class life was essentially personal.

Apart from work and the occasional election, in which all were expected to take part, impersonal relations were to be reserved for other, higher ranks. Thus in constructing a ground-level social formation for the post-war working class, Young was reproducing yet another element of wartime experience: the division between officers and men.

Young's defenders might add that he listened to working-class people. But at this time how could the British elite not listen to its own working class? They had just fought a world war together. In fact, while Young warned against social engineering implemented from on high, he was not averse to social engineering in accordance with his own vision of (how people constituted) community. This is apparent in the concluding passage of *Family and Kinship in East London*:

> Yet even when the town planners have set themselves to create communities as well as houses, they have still put their faith in buildings, sometimes speaking as though all that was necessary for neighbourhoods was a neighbourhood unit. If this were so, then there would be no harm in shifting people about the country, for what is lost could soon be regained by skilful architecture and design. But there is surely more to a community than that. The sense of loyalty to each other amongst the inhabitants of a place like Bethnal Green is not due to buildings. It is due far more to ties of kinship and friendship which connect the *people* of one household to the *people* of another. In such a district community spirit does not have to fostered, it is already there. If the authorities regard that spirit as a social asset worth preserving, they will not uproot more people but build the new houses around the social groups to which they already belong. (Young and Willmott 1957: 166, emphasis in the original)

In passages such as these, the social engineers of post-war Britain were advised to dig deep into community rather than burying it in the past. But in Young's account of it, the working class was buried in a picture of ongoing traditions which would have been better understood as only a simple part of its compound existence; not buried alive, perhaps, but resurrected in shadow rather than substance.

In Young's rendition the subtraction of all except interpersonal relations led to an idealised abstraction of social relations presented in the form of empirical data. Young was bringing the family back in. But in doing so he was writing out all those forces which had brought working people out of the family and into existence as a class – in wartime, especially, as a class acting for the nation. In that it mistook domesticity for social reality, Young's supposed gritty realism was really an idealisation of community.

During the course of his professional life, this ideal became a reality. But this does not mean that the realisation of a domesticated working class should be seen as the application of a plan hatched in advance by Young and his staff. Rather, their model of working-class life was in keeping with trends of the time. At this particular point in its history, the expansive character of British capital was going into reverse, and this diminishing movement was neatly captured in the shrinking social space of the Young model.

In short, imperial British capital was stretched to its widest-ever extent in the course of the Second World War but contracted in its aftermath. After demobilisation, while women were shepherded out of the factories back into the home, men too were expected to spend less time in public – whether in politics or in the pub. Personal relations, with all pathways leading back to the home, came to the fore, while impersonal relations were largely confined to the transactional realm of economics. This set the stage for the development of what became known as the 'consumer society', in which impersonal relations were only the means to support the intimately personal space of domestic consumption.

This contraction was characteristic of British society throughout the post-war boom and beyond. But as the boom became barely audible in the 1970s, it transpired that the reduction of politics had set yet more precedents; this time for the uncomfortable sensation of being monopolised by the market, and the consequent turn to community in the hope of enlarging personal relations to the scale of the social role previously played by the impersonal relations of politics.

ELITE MOBILISATION

In the year that he acceded (unelected) to the position of prime minister, Gordon Brown published a paean to 'Britain's everyday heroes' subtitled *The Making of the Good Society* (Brown 2007).

Introducing his book, Brown reminisced about the old ways, witnessed as a child in Kirkcaldy, of 'individuals doing their duty, communities coming together and a supportive government playing its part'. While he reports 'the fading of older ways', he claims to observe the emergence of 'new and exciting forms of civic life and social participation' facilitated by 'modern technologies' which open up 'entirely new ways for us to communicate and build new communities that support and mentor those in need' (Brown 2007: 14–15) He tells of 'communities being transformed and revived, of good people who are mentoring the young, tackling anti-social behaviour and gun crime, addressing homelessness, environmental degradation and the alienation of young people' (Brown 2007: 10).

Ostensibly, the working class is again being offered community as the means of sustainable social enrichment. But are they the only ones who are poor in heart? The increasingly fraught figure of Gordon Brown suggests otherwise; it indicates the extent to which those occupying the highest positions do not now feel at home in these positions (a kind of 'homelessness'); in their own perception of it and of the way that they themselves have held it, public office has suffered degradation; and, if New Labour is anything to go by, they are experiencing increased alienation from each other, and even from the 'young country' which they identified so strongly in the 1997 general election campaign.

In these conditions, although the idea of community tends to be applied by the elite to other people, perhaps those most in need of coming together as a community are the incoherent elite themselves. Having reduced the working class to the rubble of strictly personal relations, they themselves are a rabble army in search of a rallying point. But what should they come together around? What, rather than who, would be the basis for their communion? Theirs, after all, is the generation that made impersonal relations more difficult by taking out even the tiny amount that was left of them in politics. They removed the last traces of political solidarity in which human subjects objectified themselves in pursuit of principled objectives. As the basis for their elite community, all they have is personal relations; yet their over-reliance on personality – personal politics – is already recognised as the problem that they seek to address by coming together as a community. This is further confirmation that community, the idea of extending personal relations to the point where they constitute 'good society', exists only as an abstract idea when abstracted from the impersonal relations of which capitalist society has been primarily comprised.

Having domesticated the working class – partly through the containing idea of community – members of the British elite find themselves acting not so much as capitalists, but more like domestic servants to the international flows of capital. In their attempt to hold a concerted line against the diffusion-effect of these dynamics, they are the keenest on community. Feeling their own incoherence and the need to come together most acutely, they are feeling their way towards togetherness by discovering alleged communities everywhere and thus finding opportunities to talk the concept of community into everyday existence, including their own.

Meanwhile most non-elite people get by on a provisional mixture of impersonal relations at work and in public places, and personal relations in the home. Neither set of relations is currently satisfactory, and many of us seem to spend a lot of time and effort trying to turn each one into the other. But the relations of work and public space are not readily personalised. And when personal relations are asked to bear the load of aspirations previously located in the impersonal realm of politics, they are easily over-loaded. This is a case of mistaken ID – a mistaken attempt to identify personal and impersonal relations as if they are one and the same. Some of its origins lie in the elite identification of the working class as 'community' – a magic box of the post-war period in which impersonal relations were made to disappear among the trappings of domestic life. Now, in a forlorn attempt to reconstitute itself, the British elite would repeat this vanishing trick upon its own constituency.

NOTE

1. The swansong of the Institute of Community Studies also heralded the Young Foundation, the Institute re-named in honour of its founder. Entitled *The New East End: Kinship, Race and Conflict*, it is colloquially referred to as 'Family and Kinship Revisited'.

REFERENCES

Brown, G. (2007) *Britain's Everyday Heroes*, Edinburgh, Mainstream Publishing

Dench, G., Gavron, K. and Young, M. (2006) *The New East End: Kinship, Race and Conflict*, London, Profile Books

Young, M. and Willmott, P. (1957) *Family and Kinship in East London*, London, Institute of Community Studies/Routledge and Kegan Paul

8
Virtual Communities
Versus Political Realities

Martyn Perks

The internet has wrought massive changes in the quality of life in the west, and has the potential to bring huge benefits to the developing world. Access to ideas, publishing and information sharing, and communication with people on a global scale have all been transformed in a way unimaginable to previous generations.

Just as the world of information is steadily transforming our personal and business worlds it would seem to follow that the internet might similarly have the potential to positively affect the way that we interact. UK prime minister Gordon Brown certainly thinks so, and says, '[W]e must take advantage of new technology to make sure we open up every route to participation – not as a substitute for debate, but to deepen and widen it.'[1] However, while many accept that the growth of the internet has the *potential* to encourage more social participation and political engagement, as we shall see, its influence can have the opposite effect. One only has to think of the often cited parody of the nerdy kids around the world hidden away in their bedrooms, preferring to communicate with each other online while remaining in a state of physical solitude. The purpose of this chapter is to examine the debate and to assess the extent to which the internet can affect a positive influence on politics or might exacerbate its decline.

Over the last ten years or so, it has been suggested that information technology (IT) can play a pivotal role in repairing broken social bonds – on the one hand between citizens themselves, on the other, in rejuvenating their relationship with the political establishment. For some the internet has a vital role to play in the rehabilitation of moribund and outmoded public institutions. For others, the internet offers the possibility to circumnavigate officialdom. This group suggests that if we don't trust parliamentary politics, then we should work outside it and encourage the public to engage with each other without any need of state support or involvement.

Whichever viewpoint you take, of late, we have become obsessed with joining groups – especially online. The rapid growth of the internet worldwide, together with cheaper technology, has meant more people are able to, and are desirous of, communicating with each other online. The growth in social networking coincides with year-on-year increases in the world's internet population – estimated at around 20 per cent of the total world population.

Indeed, online social networking is a phenomenon that appears to know no limits, and thousands of websites have sprung up connecting people together in myriad ways, on every conceivable subject, hobby and interest. The biggest online social networks in the West include MySpace, Facebook and Bebo, which have massive audiences, from all ages and walks of life. Facebook, originally developed for Harvard students, is now popular with middle-class professionals. It has more than 68 million active users and an average of 250,000 new registrations each day since January 2007. And its users have created and joined more than a staggering 6 million groups.[2] However, Chinese online social networking sites like QQ make Facebook's statistics pale. In 2007 QQ had 300 million active users, generating revenues of $523 million – four times as much as Facebook.[3]

However, whether the growth of social networking, especially in the west, amounts to a rebuilding of social capital is debatable. While IT might have made forming connections between people easier, it could be argued that this phenomenon reflects merely a continuation of what people did in the real world prior to the internet, and have continued to do since. The community-building potential of the internet captures the imagination, but is it the case that its new status derives from it being the only dynamic game in town?

At a time when they are facing a general collapse in their legitimacy, politicians have talked up the potential of the internet; some of them have even taken steps to establish a personal online presence. It is no surprise then to see the likes of the former UK prime minister Tony Blair with his own Facebook page,[4] but symbolic of the crass attempts of politicians to look cool, he seems out of place – at odds with the spirit of the genre – unless he really does need more friends. For example, do we need to know that Blair's interests are: 'Spending time with [his] children, reading [mainly literary classics and biographies], watching thrillers, swimming, playing tennis and playing guitar.' The 'causes' he has signed up to (including the 'Labour Party (UK)') don't exactly inspire either. With a paltry 592 members, politics online is obviously happening elsewhere anyway. As Blair's

Facebook page illustrates, each attempt by the establishment to interact and engage with the public looks increasingly empty of content.

That said, there have been more significant online interactions between the political elite and the public. The US elections in 2004 proved pivotal. Firstly, because it illustrated to those on both sides of the Atlantic how to use the internet for electioneering; secondly, it highlighted how the supposed potential of the internet to create mass support is also its Achilles' heel. In particular, Howard Dean, a Democratic party US presidential nominee, illustrated how online mass support couldn't translate into real votes. Dean stood out and took an early lead against the mainstream candidate senator John Kerry because of a significant groundswell of grassroots support built through online social networks.

Consequently he sent shock waves through the elections with pundits on both sides of the Atlantic feverishly following Dean's progress from state to state. His early success was due to his supporters organising their own meetings (often without any official Dean sanction) using websites, including MeetUp, to decide where to meet and circulating content and agendas. However, Dean eventually lost out when his ideas came under sustained attack (Perks 2004). He failed to win over his supporters through convincing arguments, they became nothing more than fundraising fodder. They were left to conjure up their own vision of what he stood for.

In the 2008 presidential nomination elections, both Hillary Clinton and Barack Obama were much more astute in using the internet. When Clinton launched her Democratic nomination campaign online, it was inevitable that the internet would be a central feature in her continuing contest to win the Democratic party nomination. Following in the footsteps of Dean's online campaigning, Obama proved to be much more adept at using the internet to his benefit. His fundraising outstripped that of his rival by attracting large numbers of small donations – with $6.5 million raised online in just a few days (Naughton 2008).

The power of online electioneering is plain to see. Elsewhere, numerous campaign groups, charities and NGOs have also done well. On one hand, the internet is good for spreading political messages far and wide, but managing how the message is understood and interpreted is very difficult. Central to the problem is the separation of virtual and real-world spheres of influence. Online, it only takes the click of a mouse to join up to something. But that also means supporters can be anyone, and not necessarily those directly affected or even interested by the cause in question.

Therefore generating vast swathes of online support can belie the quality of support: will they come out and vote or only continue to agree at arms length? Numerous charities, campaigns and voluntary organisations have done very well and raised lots of money online, capitalising on widespread support. But that has invariably meant less need for debate and argument. Hence campaigns like Make Poverty History, which generated large amounts of support, have never had to strive too hard to convince people of their political worth.

In the UK, politicians have for a long while toyed with online politics – especially trying to encourage wider participation – in the face of widening voter apathy. This has meant more focus on rejuvenating political institutions, the public sector, even suggesting how to make parliament more relevant and interesting.[5] There is also an emphasis on participation, especially in local government and among community groups in many towns and cities. Advocates argue that connecting people online will help bridge connections between people in their local communities – even in the same blocks of flats and apartment buildings. While this might in some circumstances be a useful practicality, the problem is that, examined more broadly, the idea of using the internet to form local connections downplays the far more fruitful ways that IT can help people transcend their locality through sharing interests with people in far more complex ways. Just because they happen to live in the same street may not have anything to do with their sense of communality in any meaningful sense.

Elsewhere politicians have attempted to make more direct interventions in cyberspace, but it hasn't always proved either easy or popular. MP Tom Watson, New Labour backbencher, became the first of many to start his own weblog in 2003. Others quickly followed suit, intent on connecting with their constituents online. Watson even created a '24 hour blogathon' (Tempest 2003) hoping that by staying up all night, he and other night owls would contribute useful ideas to New Labour policy. While only a few bothered, Watson's idea generated enough publicity that subsequently influenced the government into doing something similar, and on a much larger scale. Called the 'Big Conversation', it was part website and part policy road show, whereby anyone could take part to debate the issues that they believed the government should focus on. But cynics argued at the time that neither Watson nor New Labour's attempt contributed anything towards seriously changing policy. Instead, as some noted, party officials had been 'handpicking contributors and editing out their negative comments' (Bisset and Hastings 2003).

It is clear that the drive for social engagement and participation via internet technologies is propelled by a clear political agenda, but one that seeks merely to secure participation in a technical sense, rather than a more genuine sense of actively shaping the political future. This drive for participation with the public has sometimes embarrassingly backfired. In 2006 the prime minister launched the E-Petitions website for anyone wanting to start their own petition online.[6] The idea seemed like a good one at first; however it soon turned out that critical opinion was going to proliferate and the main posting became a crusade against New Labour's road pricing policy, attracting more than 1.7 million signatories. Successful 'engagement' it might have been, but this was not what No. 10 had in mind. One unnamed minister apparently called the website's director, Tom Steinberg, a 'prat' (Geoghegan 2007) for exposing the government to not just criticism, but ridicule.

Some have argued that online petitions, online conversations and so on point towards a wider trend – moving power away from the few, including the established media, and into the public and community realm. Bill Thompson, a prominent technology commentator, argues that 'new technologies will lead to changes in the distribution of power and not merely superficial changes to political practice' (Thompson 2007). But in reality, petitions are simply a chance for many to 'let off steam', rather than to provide a coherent expression of a political opposition. The aforementioned example shows that petitions provide many with an opportunity to register their continuing disaffection with New Labour: this time over its taxation of the roads. So, for some in government, experience shows online engagement is something to be avoided, as the power to destabilise takes precedence over the possibility of connection.

On the other side of the fence, people like James Crabtree, an associate editor of *openDemocracy*, has argued that we need to go much further, bypassing traditional channels and rejecting representative politics altogether: '[T]he internet can help to improve the civic lives of ordinary people ... E-democracy should not be primarily about representation, participation, or direct access to decision makers.' Above all, it's about 'self-help' (Crabtree 2007). In bypassing the state, Crabtree ignores politics with a capital P – effectively leaving it for the domain of the few – with the rest of us left literally to sort out our own problems. 'Public investment in e-democracy', he continues, 'should be about allowing people to help themselves, their communities, and others who are interested in the same things as them.' Thus, through 'civic hacking', ordinary people can identify and act upon problems in their local communities. By solving them they must accept responsibility for their present and future actions. As if to rub salt into the wounds, Crabtree sees all of this in very therapeutic terms. He wants 'mutual aid among citizens rather than through the state' (Crabtree 2007), based on 'reciprocity'.

So, we come back full circle, to the project of rebuilding social capital. Wherever we look, it lies at the heart, not just of the liberal left, but of the entire rainbow of politics. For some it is about trying to counter deepening voter apathy and disenfranchisement with politics. For commentators such as Charles Leadbeater, it is all about rebuilding institutions from the bottom-up using 'the intelligence of thousands of people to create better solutions' (Leadbeater 2008a). For others, such as Direct Democracy,[7] a Conservative party vehicle, it's about localising power. However, creating, administering and continually motivating broad social networks is very complex, and may be done with the best intentions, but all of this is ultimately selling us short. While citizen involvement is increasingly apparent, especially online, it still remains for a large part, predominately about local, parochial, often single-issue engagement. While any active citizenry mustn't be sniffed at, you get the impression that many broader political, social and cultural problems are not addressed in these fora, as if they are 'out of bounds'. As Charles Leadbeater, author of *We-Think: The Power of Mass Creativity* (2008b) and prominent ideas-man for New Labour, puts it: '[P]eople who were once merely recipients of services become participants in planning and commissioning the services that support them' (Leadbeater 2008a). Thus, a genuine sense of political engagement is replaced by schemes to ensure participation in the technical business of running the very services that would otherwise be provided by the state or locality. Technology that is purported to expand possibilities ends up harnessing us to the kind of tasks that centralised services have previously allowed us to escape from in order to do something more useful.

In a technical sense, creating, maintaining and administering broad social networks can be time consuming and complex, and technology has a significantly beneficial impact on helping us do this successfully. However, whether technology is able to deliver anything substantially meaningful in terms of creating social engagement itself is seldom opened up to question. Many supporters of IT as the creator of virtual communities rarely question why some people are so disenfranchised with politics. Instead the growing momentum around IT tends to reinforce – rather than repair – the feeling of dislocation between the public and the political establishment. In this sense it is hardly surprising that a more meaningful use of IT is undermined.

Indeed through reinforcing various rules of etiquette and self-regulation the current use of IT often seems directly opposed to ambitious outcomes. The desire for genuine, open-ended debate that is argumentative, of opposing ideas and interests, soon gets curtailed by lawyers insisting on disclaimers and providing users with report buttons to alert moderators to remove anything deemed offensive. What is offensive is then often left for the website publisher to decide. In this sense, IT might, paradoxically, be said to hold back a genuine critical engagement in favour of promoting the need to avoid any potential for offending others within the community. Just when we have unprecedented access to ideas and information, many instead choose to worry about the consequences of unfettered debate.

Politics can unquestionably benefit from the effects of technology. But the demand for networking technology masks the fact that although we are more connected than ever, there is also a widespread sense of disconnection with political institutions. The exponential growth of online social networks must be partly due to the limitations of what is on offer elsewhere. Instead of a genuine sense of political engagement in the real world, we've decamped to chatter in the virtual world.

At the moment, the character of the debate is very much a consequence of the elite's narrow agenda and continual angst about its own marginalisation. Should a strong tradition and culture of open debate (and heated disagreements over issues and policy) remerge, then online social networking might prove very useful to involve people further. However, much of what we consider innovative technology probably wouldn't cope with a serious level of engagement and, perversely, interaction.

NOTES

1. Brown, G., 'A new kind of politics – join us', New Labour website, www4.labour.org.uk/joinus/ (accessed 1 May 2008)
2. Facebook, www.facebook.com/press/info.php?statistics/ (accessed 1 May 2008)
3. Leow, L., 'QQ, China's largest social networking site, raking in the dough', www.psfk.com/2008/03/qq-chinas-largest-social-networking-site-raking-in-the-dough.html (accessed 12 May 2008)
4. Tony Blair's Facebook profile, www.facebook.com/pages/Tony-Blair/6883528379?ref=s (accessed 18 March 2008)
5. 'Parliament in the public eye', Public Hub, Civil Service, www.nationalschool.gov.uk/policyhub/news_item/parliament_hansardsoc.asp (accessed 18 March 2008)
6. Downing Street E-Petitions, http://petitions.pm.gov.uk/ (accessed 1 May 2008)
7. Direct Democracy, www.direct-democracy.co.uk/ (accessed 1 May 2008)

REFERENCES

Bisset, S. and Hastings, C. (2003) 'Revealed: Labour's Big Conversation is a fix', *Daily Telegraph*, 29 November

Crabtree, J. (2007) 'Civic hacking: a new agenda for e-democracy', *openDemocracy*, 12 June, www.opendemocracy.net/debates/article-8-85-1025.jsp/ (accessed 1 May 2008)

Geoghegan, T. (2007) 'The petition, the "prat" and a political ideal', *BBC News Magazine*, 13 February, http://news.bbc.co.uk/1/hi/magazine/6354735.stm/ (accessed 1 May 2008)

Leadbeater, C. (2008a) 'This time it's personal', *Guardian*, 16 January

Leadbeater, C. (2008b) *We-Think: The Power of Mass Creativity*, London, Profile Books

Naughton, P. (2008) 'Hillary Clinton loan sparks online fundraising frenzy for Barack Obama', *The Times*, 7 February

Perks, M. (2004) 'Dean and not heard', *spiked*, 6 February, www.spiked-online.com/Articles/0000000CA3D5.htm/ (accessed 1 May 2008)

Tempest, M. (2003) 'Parliament goes wireless for bloggers' summit', *Guardian*, 14 July

Thompson, B. (2007) 'The political power of the network', *BBC News* website, 27 February, http://news.bbc.co.uk/1/hi/technology/6400337.stm/ (accessed 1 May 2008)

9

Minorities, Multiculturalism and the Metropolitan Experience

Neil Davenport

In recent years, multiculturalism has been seen as a positive and modern advance on the coercive practices against ethnic minorities that were commonplace in the 1970s and 1980s. However, I contend that multiculturalism represents the failure to provide access to adequate resources to all citizens and institutionalises false and ultimately divisive notions of 'difference'. The purpose of this chapter is to explain how these retrograde trends developed in urban policy and development.

For the past thirty years, urban policy and development has been guided by multiculturalism; the belief that humans are permanently localised into different cultural belongings that must be respected, tolerated and even nurtured.

This application of multiculturalism has largely taken on two broad approaches. Throughout the 1980s, it was used effectively as a form of social control against ethnic minorities angry at their bitter experiences of racism in British society. More recently, multiculturalism has come to be seen as a way to re-brand local communities and thus give a sheen of positive identification to once 'down at heel' areas. Hence 'culture' in and of itself is regularly thought of as having beneficial and transformative effects on urban development.

IDENTITY POLITICS

In the 1960s and 1970s, a number of left-wing intellectuals began to question and challenge the notions of reason, progress and universalism. These challenges coalesced into an outlook that popularly became known as postmodernism. In brief, writers such as Fredric Jameson and Jacques Derrida, characterised the 'postmodern age' as the fragmentation of society into multiple, incommensurable forms of human life; and according to the French thinker Jean-François Lyotard, this means that any attempt to understand and describe, in their totality, the laws of development of human society is impossible (Lyotard 1989: xxiv). Such 'meta-narratives' (meaning an over-arching framework) are problematic because, postmodernists argued, they tend to eradicate differences and thus impose a rigid uniformity on humanity.

Tariq Modood, a sociologist and an expert on British Muslims, believes there is a connection between the emergence of postmodern ideas and an increased 'Muslim assertiveness', that is, the demand that Muslims be recognised as a 'distinct group' (Modood 2005: 153). He believes that modernist conceptions of 'liberal equality' have been 'supplanted by the concept of equality of difference' (Modood 2005: 153). What Modood is referring to is Michel Foucault's belief that instead of there being a universal agent to liberate humanity, there is, he suggests, a 'plurality of resistances' (Foucault 1990: 153) such as the various black protest groups in America during the 1960s. By linking black liberation with the celebration of ethnic identity, the Black Power Movement marked a broader shift towards identity politics among radical groups. Modood suggests that 'Asian groups, including Muslims, borrowed the logic of ethnic pride and tried to catch up with the success of a newly legitimised black identity' (Modood, 2005: 157).

It is plausible to suggest that Black nationalism spurred on ideas of separatism and 'difference' for other ethnic groups. However, it was the western elites' growing unease with their own claims to universalism that created an opening for particularistic identities to flourish (Furedi 1992: 234) and for that to permeate through into urban policy and development. In 1966, the then Labour government's home secretary, Roy Jenkins, insisted that the government did not 'seek a flattening process of uniformity, but cultural diversity' (Mason 1995). It was this rejection of universalism in favour of multiculturalism that encouraged ethnic minorities to demand that their distinct cultures and values should be catered for in urban policy.

Assertions of particular ethnic identities in Britain first emerged in Bradford in the early 1970s. Previously, the majority of post-war immigrants from the South Asian continent had been migrant workers. However, the 1971 Immigration Act for example, coinciding with the break-up of Pakistan, tightened the rules and stopped immigration for single men. It forced many workers from Pakistan to become settlers rather than sojourners, with the arrival of wives, fiancées and children, which 'created a need for mosques and religious teachers' (Lewis 2002: 127). A seminal article on Bradford's Pakistani community, based on research in the early 1970s, outlined a two-stage process of community formation. Firstly, it was argued that there was an initial tendency towards integration which gave way to segmentation as numbers grew (cited in Lewis 2002: 129). Secondly, the 'bottom up' process implies that Muslim pressure then led to a proliferation of mosques and supplementary schools, reflecting, it was argued, 'a determination to pass on the Islamic tradition to their children and grandchildren' (Lewis 2002: 62). This scenario suggests that there is something inherent *within* Islamic beliefs that facilitates segregationist demands. But is it the case that state institutions simply 'gave in' to demands for cultural recognition?

In a Bradford council report of 1981, the author concluded that there had been 'settlement by tiptoe' from South Asian Muslims with a desire 'to preserve their traditional culture, religion and language' (Lewis 2002: 97). This was reflected in the formation of Bradford Council of Mosques in September 1981, which campaigned mainly on educational issues and according to Lewis and Raza, they were to prove highly influential. So much so that by 1982, Bradford education authority had issued guidelines to schools – 'Education for a Multi-cultural Society: Provisions for Pupils of Ethnic Minority Communities' – intended to accommodate Muslim cultural and religious needs 'within one educational system'. The cooperative manner of the Bradford Council of Mosques was rewarded by Bradford's Local Education Authority (LEA) in 1983, with halal meat provided in schools for the district's 15,000 Muslim pupils.

Faced with growing militancy, Bradford council drew up a twelve-point race relations plan, declaring that every section of the 'multiracial, multicultural city' had 'an equal right to maintain its own identity, culture, language, religion and customs'. In 1981 'the council helped set up and fund the Bradford Council of Mosques' as well as instituting 'other religious umbrella groups for Sikhs and Hindus' (Lewis 2002: 3). The outcome was that by the mid-1980s 'the focus of anti-racist protest in Bradford had shifted from political issues, such as policing and immigration, to religious and cultural issues' (Lewis 2002: 3). For race academics Kenan Malik and Pnina Werbner, such moves are examples of local authorities cynically promoting 'identity politics', as a way of controlling 'frequent conflicts between Asian youth, racist organisations and the police' (Malik 2002: 3).

Pnina Werbner's account of the Asian Youth Movement (AYM) in Bradford makes a similar point. The AYM was founded in 1978 as a pan-Asian, anti-racist youth movement transcending Hindu, Sikh and Muslim communal identities. Compared to the particularist ethos of the Bradford Council of Mosques, AYM was built on the assumption that racial discrimination ran parallel to, and thus reinforced, 'the better-known structures of class inequality ... with (blacks/Asians) the victims of "exclusion" from urban policy' (Werbner 1997: 129). It was the establishment of Council-sponsored Muslim, Sikh and Hindu community centres that, it was argued, divided 'pan-Asian unity'. As a consequence, the AYM 'couldn't survive the centrifugal pull of these religious identities' (Werbner 1997: 129). For Malik, this had little to do with the potency of identity; the tensions between different Asian communities only emerged as each fought for a greater allocation of council funding (Malik 2002: 8). Such measures also had a tendency to sidestep further demands coming from these sections of the community. Another report by Bradford council noted that its multicultural initiatives had succeeding in narrowing the horizons of Asian activists: 'There is now a greater appreciation amongst ethnic minorities of both the limitations of the local authority and its powers. Expressions

of demand are now more realistic and well thought out'
(Thompson 1988: 61).

What makes the arguments put forward by Malik and
Werbner convincing is that a similar process, of ethnic
containment through multicultural urban policy, was being
established in other cities throughout the UK. In particular,
as many inner cities in Britain erupted and as blacks and
Asians rioted, angered by racial discrimination and police
harassment, diffusing such bitterness and resentment became
a political priority. The multicultural strategy facilitated the
implementation of token measures, for example over language
and customs, while leaving systematic inequalities in place.

MUNICIPAL MULTICULTURALISM

The inner-city riots of 1981 led the then Conservative administration to set up the Urban Programme and that year £7.5
million of its money went to cultural and employment projects
involving black people. By 1984/85 this figure had risen to
£27.6 million and by 1986 to £38.8 million (Thompson 1988:
100). Britain's local authorities were, by law, required to
'make special provision ... in consequence of the presence
within their areas of substantial numbers of immigrants from
the Commonwealth'. Militant black activists saw the Urban
Programme as a mechanism to encourage blacks to acquiesce
to the government's demands. Rather than urban policy being
based on universal principles of equal citizenship, and an
equal access to the resources created by development; the
Conservative government's specific targeting of black people
effectively treated them as second-class citizens – victims
dependent on charity – precisely what activists were protesting

against. Indeed, the failure of these projects was confirmed by the further riots and disturbances in September 1985. As they were viewed by many as the party of empire, the Conservatives had little success in cultivating a black middle class and could make no headway with black militants.

Fortunately for the Conservatives' publicity machine, nation-wide black uprisings coincided with the establishment of radical Labour councils in many inner-city areas. They were ripe for parody. The left-wing activists who dominated the new councils were, in the main, committed on paper to a policy of fighting racism. As almost half of Britain's black population was, and still is, concentrated in London, this became the key arena for municipal multiculturalism. Herman Ousley of the Greater London Council promised to 'introduce an ethnic dimension into policy-making procedures', and to appoint 'ethnic advisers' to see through 'black self-help' initiatives (Thompson 1988: 101). But for all the talk of equal opportunity in Ousley's programme, the compartmentalising of black and Asian people as being in need of greater cultural recognition succeeded only in caricaturing them as unequal citizens.

Activists grew dependent on council grants, resources and facilities to maintain their momentum. Often such grants were based on demanding cultural recognition, rather than demanding political equality. It was not so much that radical activists were bought off (though some undoubtedly were), but rather that their whole outlook was being shaped by what had become an industry – the 'multiculturalism industry'. The effects of nearly a decade of multicultural policies can be seen in the response to the Salman Rushdie's *The Satanic Verses* (1988). Radical Muslims, who'd previously campaigned for equal treatment were now publicly burning copies of the novel on the grounds that it was 'blasphemous'. They demanded that the law be changed to protect Muslims from such an offence against their sensibilities.

By the early 1990s, traditional sources of national identity were no longer adequate to provide a focus for unity in an increasingly fragmented, 'postmodern' society. John Major's lame evocation of warm beer and cricket only served to confirm the exhaustion of traditional sources of elite authority. It was in this context that multiculturalism graduated from municipal local politics to the very centre stage of British life. Multiculturalism seemed to provide an alternative foundation on which to build social cohesion.

The writer on race politics, Paul Gilroy, has noted that multiculturalism flourished as an opportunist strategy to resolve the British establishment's crisis of legitimacy (Gilroy 2004: 58). It is not only a key policy theme for New Labour, but has been signed up to by all sections of the British establishment. In the wake of the McPherson report (published in 1999 in the wake of the Stephen Lawrence murder), even the so-called 'institutionally racist' police force (the very institution that a decade earlier had been at the forefront of repressing black unrest), embraced cultural diversity. It was after these findings that multiculturalism became the official ideology and the key practice within urban policy. Furthermore, whereas multiculturalism was once about the containment of ethnic minorities, nowadays it is regarded as a regenerative force that might transform Britain's inner cities.

MULTICULTURALISM AND 'URBAN RENAISSANCE'

The economic upturn in the late 1990s laid the material basis for regeneration and gentrification of many of Britain's inner cities. The emphasis on 'secure neighbourhoods', modelled on New York mayor Rudy Giuliani's controversial 'zero-tolerance' policy, also led many to view cities with increased optimism (Heartfield 2006: 107). The enthusiasm for cultural diversity as an aid to urban regeneration, especially in London, can be seen as another factor in the much-heralded urban renaissance. So whereas the existence of ethnic minorities was a cause for alarm for conservatives in the 1980s; by the late 1990s the diversity of the inner city was an important part of the re-branding of what were once considered down-at-heel areas.

Of course, this is not to gloss over concerns raised at the time – and since – that Britain is 'sleepwalking into segregation' as Trevor Phillips of the Commission for Racial Equality put it (*Guardian* 2005); or that, post-9/11 and especially post-7/7, some Muslim-dominated areas such as Bradford and Oldham have become isolated from wider society, and could potentially be a source of conflict and instability. Increasingly multiculturalism is put in the dock for nurturing ethnic grievances, exacerbating alienation of Muslim and black youth, and acting as a poor substitute for social cohesion. But actually, every step of the way, the perceived solution to the problems, problems that have been generated by multiculturalism, is a call for *greater diversity*. For example, Phillips calls for ethnic quotas in areas that are largely made up of one social group. This is intended to break down the barriers caused by ghettoisation, but by categorising residents according to ethnicity it institutionalises – and draws attention to – difference (Davenport 2005).

In a similar vein, Ash Amin's report on ethnicity and urban policy initially paints a grim picture of patchwork communities living cheek-by-jowl, sometimes spilling out into conflict as in

Oldham and Bradford in 2001. But then the author champions the 'very real cultural dynamism that is to be found within ethnic minority communities' (Amin 2002: 7) as a solution to segregation. 'In Leicester the year is punctuated with events that are celebrated by one community but enjoyed by all', says Amin. 'These include Council-supported celebrations for Eid, Hannuka, the Leicester Caribbean carnival, Diwali, an Asian Mela or fair', he continues (Amin 2002: 8). Another report describes a Leicester of multi-ethnic areas where schools 'are the best performing in the city and that they help combat racist stereotypes, while leading pupils to the acceptance that the world they live in is made up of very different individuals' (Semprebon 2004: 12). In other words, rather than the authorities having to deal with diversity in urban areas, diversity is now seen as the official policy solution for a number of alleged social ills.

The London district of Hackney, for instance, is praised for its cultural mix, with a 48 per cent ethnic minority resident population, made up of 23 ethnic groups speaking 37 different languages, each contributing to the development of an 'atmosphere characterised by liveliness, diversity and tolerance' (Koutrolikou 2004: 7). As a result, 'Hackney's reputation has changed dramatically from being a slum into being London's new cultural Mecca with plenty of galleries, bars, lofts and international "creatives"' (Koutrolikou 2004: 7). Those who live there may not recognise the spin.

Likewise Brick Lane in East London was once seen as the exemplification of racial tension, poverty and urban decline. Now, the area's large Bangladeshi community – with their assorted shops, markets and restaurants – has given it a 'vibrant' feel and the area is thus re-branded as 'modern and multicultural' and a desirable place to live. Whereas Tower

Hamlets in the 1980s effectively created ghettos of poverty-stricken Asians, now the area is seen as a model of diversity, multiculturalism and regeneration.

However, the primacy of culture relegates the self-interested individual acting in the public sphere, i.e. the citizen. In secular states, the private spheres of personal life and religious and cultural practices are seen as separate to the public spheres of work, politics and citizenship. Multiculturalism makes no such distinction, relating to ethnic minorities as communities who are defined only in terms of these private, cultural spheres. If the public sphere is not seen as culturally or ethnically neutral, it becomes legitimate for immigrant groups' particular identities to be recognised over and above their status as citizens (Modood 2005: 137).

Of course, the persistence of social inequalities and racial discrimination calls into question how fair society is. Nevertheless, we should be arguing for the application of universal standards of rights, liberties and equality, not the primacy of difference. After all, the 'equality of difference' is a contradiction in terms.

CONCLUSION

Over a thirty-year period, the ethos of multiculturalism has been at the heart of urban policy in Britain. Responding to angry demands for equal treatment and an end to racial discrimination, urban policy makers found it far easier to encourage ethnic minorities to seek redress in terms of cultural recognition rather than equal citizenship. No longer just an attempt to buy off unruly black and Asian people in inner cities, multiculturalism has been rebranded as a youthful, modern and engaging way of bringing people of all cultures together. Cultural diversity is now a key theme in the project of urban renaissance in Britain's inner cities. But privileging ethnic minorities' particular and private cultural identities is to continue to deny them social equality, and by so doing, it undermines any meaningful prospect of a unified community.

REFERENCES

Amin, A. (2002) 'Ethnicity and the multicultural city: living with diversity', report for the ESRC CITIES Programme and the Department of Transport, Local Government and the Regions, January

Calcutt, A. (09.2007) 'Culture and anomie', *Rising East-Online*, www.uel.ac.uk/risingeast/archive07/academic/calcutt.htm

Davenport, N. (2005) 'Trevor Phillips: ghetto blaster?', s*piked*, 20 September, www.spiked-online.com/index.php?/site/article/573/ (accessed 1 May 2007)

Derrida, J. (1974) *Of Grammatology*, Johns Hopkins University Press

Furedi, F. (1992) *Mythical Past, Elusive Future: History and Society in an Anxious Age*, Pluto Press

Gilroy, P. (2004) *After Empire: Multiculture or Postcolonial Melancholia*, Routledge

Guardian (2005) 'Britain "sleepwalking to segregation"', 19 September

Heartfield, J. (2006) *Let's Build: Why We Need Five Million New Homes in the Next 10 Years*, London, Audacity

Koutrolikou, P. (2004) 'Negotiating "common grounds" through local government and urban regeneration policies and initiatives; the case of Hackney, London' (paper)

Lewis, P. (1994) *Islamic Britain: Religion, Politics and Identity among British Muslims*, I. B. Tauris

Lyotard, J. (1989) *The Postmodern Condition: A Report On Knowledge*, Manchester University Press

Mason, D. (1995) *Race & Ethnicity in Modern Britain*, Oxford University Press

Malik, K. (1989) 'Dewsbury after Rushdie', *Living Marxism*, May

Malik, K. (2002), 'Multiculturalism is divisive', *New Humanist*, summer

Modood, T. (2005) *Multicultural Politics: Racism, Ethnicity and Muslims in Britain*, Edinburgh University Press

Modood, T. and Werbner, P. (1997) *The Politics of Multiculturalism in the New Europe: Racism, Identity and Community*, Zed

Semprebon, M. (2004), *Managing Diversity: Rotterdam and Leicester Compared*, Research and Training Network

Thompson, K. (1988) *Under Siege: Racial Violence in Britain Today*, Penguin

10

From Little Italy to Big America

Elisabetta Gasparoni-Abraham

As you approach North Beach today, the road sign for Little Italy is imposing, green, and proudly features a map of Italy. This neighbourhood has its roots deep in the soil of West Coast Italian immigrant history. Little Italy today, however, exists mainly as a tourist attraction, a feeling of 'romantic Italy'. The Italian community of North Beach is no longer there. The history of Italian settlers in San Francisco is different from the more well-known examples of Chicago and other cities on the East Coast, but you have to dig deep in the historic chronicle of San Francisco to get to know their story.

Let us consider that even though Italians came together as a nation in 1861, they still did not have a national identity because of a strong regionalism and the lack of a common language. The unification of the Italian liberal state, rather than unifying, divided its people further and further by giving privileges to some regions and reducing the rest of them to colonies. The Italian government was the costliest in Europe and in its quest for military might and its drive to have factories at all costs, it neglected agricultural innovations and lost sight of the fact that its people were living in misery. This social, economic and political system proved unable to absorb so many differences and generated a multitude of people without political power (only 9 per cent were allowed to vote) and adequate employment. Italians started leaving their regions and many moved to the East Coast of the United States.

By 1890 the number of Italians residing in San Francisco equalled the number in Chicago but twenty years later there were three times as many Italians in Chicago. Whereas San Francisco had already seen its greatest railroad-building period, Chicago was just then on its way to transforming into the biggest railroad city in the country and needed labourers. However, too many Italians arrived: Chicago found it impossible to absorb the influx and pushed them into many other areas of the city. The Italian settlement in Chicago took a different turn.

By the time the first Italians reached the San Francisco area, at the end of the 1840s, they decided that they were going to stay for good. Italy was so far away and the opportunities they had here seemed abundant. However, they understood that in order to survive the hardship of their status as outsiders, they needed to stick together to defend their interests and pool their resources.

By 1850, three years after a Catholic Mission, a military fort and an area comprised of a couple of ranches and a few shops were christened San Francisco; only 35 Italians lived in the city. We don't know much about them except that Italians had left Italy because they were looking for a better life (or because they were Republicans intent on fleeing their monarchist homeland). Although it was principally gold that attracted them, very soon they gave up the gold miners' life and settled down as merchants, clerks, labourers, boarding house keepers, sailors, bartenders (and of course a priest) in this booming town. Even though the total population of San Francisco at this point was only about 800, it is worth noting that in the next eight years it grew to a staggering 50,000, a number that took Boston 200 years and Philadelphia 125 years to achieve! Although Italians continued to settle in San Francisco and helped to boost the growing population, few had achieved the financial rewards that had brought them there in the first place.

In 1865 the consul, Gian B. Cerruti, wrote that the Italian community in San Francisco was not as wealthy as was commonly believed abroad:

> Many of his countrymen enticed by the relentless exaggerations of a paid press, far from finding the promised land, they were obliged to take on arduous, poorly paid, unsteady work; but unable to back out, resigned themselves to their fate. Many could not endure the hardship involved in their quest and perished in the mountains; others fell victim to the daggers of bandits and the arrows of Indians. A few for whom fortune has been less grim prepared to return to Italy to enjoy the fruits of their labour only to contract diseases which robbed them of their savings and their health, medical care being very poor in these inhospitable places. (Canepa and Baccari 1981/82)

It was precisely because of the precarious conditions they were living in, and in order to guarantee medical assistance for themselves and their families, that the Italians who had settled in an area of San Francisco called North Beach decided to open a hospital. This possibility of mutual support did not last, however, because the conflicts that had originated in Italy were also a part of the identity they brought with them. Their regional differences and distrusts were the greatest obstacles to the creation of a community in North Beach.

Garibaldi's prophecy about Italians 'falling out of the ranks' was becoming even more apparent by the late 1870s. At that point San Francisco's Italians finally got down to concentrating on what they could do for themselves in this country. They began to set aside their old difficulties and set anew to truly build a community. From 1895 to 1917 they took the time to consolidate their growing position in the city. During this period four Italian banks and four newspapers were established. A.P. Giannini's Bank of Italy (now Bank of America) had become the largest in the state of California. North Beach (by now also called the Italian Colony) took a leading role in the reconstruction of the city after the earthquake and fire of 1906 (after four days of fire no more than three buildings were left standing!). Alongside the growing affluence of Italians in the wine industry, all of this contributed to the Italians' upward mobility. The barbers, butchers, bakers, fishermen and farmers all deposited their savings in Italian-owned banks. That money came back to them in the form of loans with which to purchase shops, fishing boats, homes, bakeries and farms.

Such economic achievement was an exception among Italians in America. Elsewhere in the US the distrust that originated in the homeland tended to block their ability to organise activities effectively. The mutual benefit societies springing up in other Italian communities were formed of individuals from the same town or more often from the same parish. Others were not admitted. Although capital resources may have existed among wealthy New York or Chicago Italians, these remained mostly underutilised for the benefit of a strong, cohesive community. Italians everywhere else in America were considered rag-pickers, peanut vendors or gangsters. As San Francisco was such a young and resourceful city, it was not necessary to stay outside of the law. The criminal element was not as entrenched as in Chicago or New York, and it was possible for the Italian immigrants to build a strong power base. They did it so well that in 1931 an Italian was elected mayor of San Francisco.

Although these Italian migrants saw that favourable articles on Little Italy were being written, they knew that their status in the city and America more broadly was still the one of a second-class citizen. They did not consider themselves totally integrated into American society. There were too few Italians who could speak English and even if their standard of living equalled that of Americans, many of their jobs were still blue collar. However, a movement that was growing stronger and stronger in Italy seemed to address their concerns. Fascist influence grew very strong in North Beach. It was thought that Mussolini might help in defining finally what Italians were about. Added to this, many of the colony's businessmen depended on trade relations with Italy, and thus needed import permits from Rome. The incentive to keep on the right side of the fascists in power back home was a strong one.

By the mid-1930s, however, Senator William Borah, a key political figure of the time, declared that no one who advocated or believed in fascism could claim to be a loyal American citizen. This was a clear message to the Italians in the US. Fascism had reawakened old polarities in the San Francisco Italian community. Those who used to be Republican were now anti-fascist, and those who used to be pro-monarchy were now supporting fascism. But Little Italy was still the Italian enclave, home to the immigrants that came from Italy; and the battle was largely confined to articles published in a handful of Italian newspapers rather than activism on the streets of Little Italy.

However, when the Second World War broke out, 600,000 Italians were classified as enemy aliens. Many lost their livelihoods because of curfew restrictions, and in some cases their business were boycotted. Italians across America, and certainly in North Beach, supported the US. In so doing, they asserted themselves as equals and their identity as Italian-Americans grew stronger and stronger. The conflict wiped away the belief that fascism could help formulate an identity around which the Italians of San Francisco might cohere.

With this, the North Beach Italian community began to wither. The Italian colony's ultimate function was to be assimilated. In the late 1950s, the Italians in North Beach started to move out and to integrate with the wider society of which they were a part. Their banks became American banks; their wineries saturated the local market; and their politicians, having won the colony's every vote, were now seeking broader constituencies. The very success of the community led inevitably to its demise. The Italian colony of North Beach no longer exists in any meaningful sense. The imposing road sign for Little Italy on the approach to North Beach is all that remains; the community that was has become something else.

Sometimes the people I meet here in San Francisco with North Beach origins still have Italian family names. But their first names have been Americanised, they do not speak Italian, and they *feel* American. I met a retired teacher who grew up in North Beach in the 1940s. Her father was an orphan from Cuba and her mother a third generation Italian. She grew up in what she calls an Italian community: 'Everybody knew each other, people spoke Italian', she recalls. 'It truly felt like being in a small corner of the mother country! All of that does not exist anymore, now North Beach is Chinese, American, Argentinean and Filipino!'

For the people of San Francisco today, Little Italy is a neighbourhood that is defined not just by the presence of pizzerias and restaurants serving Italian food, or cafés, delicatessen shops and bakeries with Italian names. Indeed, the American Planning Association has proclaimed North Beach one of the ten Great Neighbourhoods in America on account of its social mix, and the great diversity of ownership and architectural styles. Little Italy is not even mentioned.

There is no longer an Italian community in North Beach; the conditions that gave rise to it at the turn of the last century have faded. Little Italy only lives on in nostalgia for a past long gone. The Italian coffeehouses and restaurants are for tourists more than the people who live or work nearby. North Beach today is known equally well for designer clothing boutiques. You are more likely to find Asian immigrants doing tai chi in Washington Square (North Beach's main square) than Italian men sitting on benches smoking. Here you can also find Lawrence Ferlinghetti's City Lights Bookstore, the Caffe Trieste and the Cellar Jazz Bar. These are the places where the beat poets Jack Kerouac, Allen Ginsberg, Michael McClure, Gary Snider, Philip Whalen and Philip Lamantia hung out in the late 1950s, gaining public exposure and notoriety. This is where people continue to come together and feel they belong, a feeling rooted in a shared interest and experience of living in the wider metropolitan community.

BIBLIOGRAPHY

Research from the San Francisco Central Library Archives and the Italian Institute

Borelli, K. (1965) *U.S. Immigration Policy with Particular Reference to the Reactions of the San Francisco Italian Community*, senior thesis, San Luis Obispo, California State Polytechnic College

Canepa, A.M. and Baccari, A. (Winter 1981/82) 'The Italians of San Francisco in 1865: G.B. Cerruti's report to the Ministry of Foreign Affairs', *California History*, Vol. 60, No. 4, pp. 350–69

Cinel, D. (1983) *From Italy to San Francisco: The Immigrant Experience*, Stanford, Stanford University Press

Dondero, C. (1983) *Societa' Italiana di Mutua Beneficenza*, Colma, S.I.M.B.

Firpo, T. (1983–1984) 'La Comunita' Italiana di San Francisco', unpublished doctoral thesis, Universita' di Genova, Facolta' di Lettere e Filosofia

Fischera, S. (1981) *The Meaning of Community: A History of Italians of San Francisco*, Los Angeles, University of California Press

Fondazione, G.A. (1980) *The Italian-Americans: Who They Are, Where They Live, How Many They Are*, Turin, Fondazione Giovanni Agnelli

Grossman, P.R. (1966) *The Italians in America*, Minneapolis, Lerner Publications Company

Guerin, D. (1975) *Il Movimento Operaio Negli Stati Uniti 1867–1970*, Roma, Editori Riuniti

The Italian Catholic Federation Heritage Book Committee (1994) *Our Italian-American Heritage*, Merced, California, Polito Printers

LoGatto, Reverend A.F. (1972) *The Italians in America 1492–1972*, New York, Oceana Publications, INC

Margariti, A. (1979) *America! America!* Casalvelino Scalo, SA, Galzerano Editore

Paoli Gumina, D. (1978) *Gli Italiani di San Francisco 1850–1930*, New York, Center for Migration Studies

Rolle, F.A. (1972) *Gli Emigrati Vittoriosi*, Verona, Arnoldo Mondadori Editore

Sensi-Isolana, P.A. and Cancilla Martinelli, P. (1993) *Struggle and Success. An Anthology of the Italian Immigrant Experience in California*, New York, CMS

11
Rio on Galway:
Immigration and Ireland

Suzy Dean

In the early 1990s, Gort, a small community in County Galway, Ireland, was little more than a ghost town. The population of this agricultural town had been declining gradually since 1830, but with hardly any local industry to speak of and shops closing, younger generations were leaving in droves (*Irish Times* 2007a).

In 1999, however, something happened to reverse Gort's decline. An influx of Brazilian migrants into the meat industry became the unexpected catalyst for this change. When Jerry O'Callaghan, the manager of a local meat-processing factory – Kepak – became concerned about a lack of skilled workers in Ireland, he decided to look to the Brazilian meat business with which he had established links in the late 1970s. 'The first [Brazilian worker] came to Kepak [and] we saw that work permits could be had in Ireland. So in 1998 we ... sent over the first 25' (Mac Cormaic 2007). Seeing Kepak's success, other Irish factories suffering similar labour shortages started recruiting from the same pool of skilled workers in Anápolis in Goias, Brazil (Mac Cormaic 2007). The Goias region has a huge meat industry – even though it is also the most populous of Brazil's central regions, there are reportedly four cows to every (human) resident!

While the Irish connection with Brazil originated with the shortage of Irish slaughterhouse and meat-processing workers, it also depended on a surfeit of workers in Brazil. The enormous factory in Anápolis, which until the late 1990s was the largest local employer, became a victim of the slump in meat exports (Mac Cormaic 2007).

Since the arrival of the first Brazilians in 1999 there has been a population explosion in Gort. The number of inhabitants has once again returned to its early twentieth-century peak. According to the 2006 Census, 40 per cent of Gort residents are non-Irish, and of these 83 per cent are Brazilian. These new residents have improved the economic standing of the community as a whole, with many of the shops that had closed now reopening. The Brazilian workers no longer occupy only the meat factories but have also taken up jobs in local stores and beauty parlours. All in all, this makes Gort one of the fastest growing towns in the west of Ireland with new housing estates springing up, and a proliferation of cafés and restaurants. The wave of Brazilian migrants now occupies around 40 per cent of the houses in Gort (*Irish Times* 2007a).

Most marked of all, perhaps, is the manner in which the new cultural dynamic in Gort has been embraced by both migrants and the established residents of the town alike. One South American news site described how 'Brazilian flags hang from pubs, posters in Portuguese advertise the agricultural fair and the vibrant green-and-yellow paintwork of the "Real Brazil" food store stands out in a drab row of shops' (Hoskins 2006). According to one Irish local, Brazilians 'have been well received by the local community and have made a positive and valuable contribution to the area. A once quiet rural Irish market town has been transformed by the colours, emotions and sounds of South America' ('Brazilian Festival in Gort' 2006). The annual celebration of the Brazilian Quadrilha festival alongside more traditional Irish fare is testament to this rich cultural mix.

Although some language difficulties remain, the Brazilian migrants are highly integrated, as everything from cooking, dancing and language tips are exchanged between the various members of the community. All this, despite Gort's long-standing cultural homogeneity. Poignantly, in spite of many only intending to stay for a short while – that is, long enough to earn sufficient money to support their families and return home – many Brazilians liked Gort so much that they have brought their families over. The predominance of one-way migration suggests a happy unity of the 'native' Irish and Brazilian migrants. Furthermore, emerging trends are indicating moderate levels of intermarriage between the two cultures, further reinforcing community integration.

However, one of the most intriguing aspects of Gort's Brazilian influx is the confusion and questioning as to why migrants and nationals are able to cohabitate peacefully.

According to Frank Murray, a Portuguese-speaking Scot, working in Gort for a community project run by the National University of Ireland in Galway, the Irish have adapted to Brazilian migration because many locals feel empathy towards the newcomers – not least on account of Ireland's long history of economic migration (Hoskins 2006). Though this no doubt plays a part, it is unlikely that history alone can explain contemporary attitudes towards migration in Gort. In 2004, a referendum resulted in migrant children born in Ireland no longer being able to acquire Irish status unless one of their parents was already an Irish citizen (*BBC News* 2004). Given this apparent hostility to migrants there appears to be no predisposed 'pro-migration' sentiment.

Other locals (Hoskins 2006) have put the easy integration of Brazilians down to an absence of ghettoisation, and the age mix (i.e. the *range* of ages included in the immigrant labour) of the Brazilians settling in Gort. Yet there is no obvious reason why a broad or indeed a narrow demographic would be particularly conducive to integration. Furthermore, ghettoisation is not unknown in Gort. There has been no shortage of stories from the migrants of Gort about poor pay and the exploitation of those unable to speak English (*Irish Times* 2007a).

In Ireland, as in many western European countries, general hostility towards immigration, fostered by politicians and the press, prevails in the public sphere (Myers 2007). Many reports about Gort express a barely concealed incredulity that the populace are living peacefully together. But if they *expect* catastrophe is it any wonder they are surprised by camaraderie, or peaceful co-existence between the residents of Gort, old and new?

A spokesperson from the Irish Centre for Migration Studies at University College Cork argues that Ireland must think seriously about how it incorporates new arrivals. Apparently 'the result of inaction now will be a form of forced, resented and almost certainly failed de facto assimilation over time' (*Irish Times* 2007b). This implies that integration is not something that should be left to communities to get on with themselves. Irish policy makers (in contrast with their UK equivalents) don't like to talk about multiculturalism, thinking it too *laissez-faire*, risking discrimination and racism.

Instead they advocate 'interculturalism', a state-led forging of links between different cultural groups. According to Philip Watt, Director of the National Consultative Committee on Racism and Interculturalism in Ireland, 'Developing a more inclusive, intercultural society is about inclusion by design, not as an afterthought' (Milly 2003).

However, multiculturalism is problematic, not because it leaves communities alone, but because it endorses the notion that there exist irreconcilable differences between cultural, ethnic and religious groups. This engenders divisions and creates tensions, fixing identity at the level of the superficial: race, religion and culture. By promoting these differences as the defining characteristics of people they are erected as insurmountable obstacles to real equality.

Interculturalism, really just a subspecies of multiculturalism, presents the same problem. Despite the emphasis on interaction there is an implicit idea that left to their own devices communities will not interact. There is an assumption that people are automatically inclined to be hostile towards immigrants. The very presence of people different from that of the host group becomes a cause for concern.

In 2004, Taiwo Matthew chose to stand in the local elections to highlight the way that, in his opinion, 'the immigrant community was being misconceived ... the one thing that breeds prejudice is not knowing anything about each other' (Fottrell 2007). Setting aside the fact that Matthew was in the end elected (demonstrating that the culture gap between immigrants and nationals is by no means unbridgeable), his thinking clearly demonstrates the problematic manner in which multiculturalism has contributed to the immigration discussion. That is to say, multiculturalism assumes that members of a culture share the same interests and characteristics, characteristics that are inherently different from the host country and inevitably problematic without the authorities' support and official mediation.

What is revealing about the situation in Gort is the disparity between people's lived experience of immigration where the established population simply get on with engaging with new locals, and the anxious nature of the wider public discussion, which frets about the problems that immigrants can cause. On the one hand, new immigrants find themselves welcomed into the immediate community, while on the other, a majority vote to reduce immigrant rights. Following the 2004 referendum on immigration status, the Irish government launched *Planning for Diversity: The National Action Plan Against Racism* (Department of Justice, Equality and Law Reform 2005). This explicitly rejects an approach that treats minorities the same as the majority of the population, institutionalising a complex system for incorporating diversity into all areas of public service provision. Both the government's decision to stage a referendum on the issue of citizenship, and the provisions of *Planning for Diversity*, serve only to perpetuate community tension. By racialising migrants and introducing a special law for them, rather than allowing them to integrate and live by the same rules as their neighbours in Gort, divisions were institutionalised.

It seems that the policy and rhetoric of multiculturalism, and the broader hostility towards immigration, has had little impact in Gort. The lived experience of immigration is of a different quality from that projected by the ruling elites. Furthermore, unlike other towns and cities in Ireland, the process of migration was not overseen by local policy makers. There *was* no policy on integration or multiculturalism in 1999. Gort's ethnographic landscape could change fairly rapidly without official typecasting of the new Brazilian migrants. Ironically, Gort is now a flagship for other communities on how integration should work (Hoskins 2006). It is showcased as an integrative success by politicians, despite the fact that it was precisely the lack of political interference that facilitated the smooth integration of the new arrivals into the community. Gort has even seen the introduction of GRACE (www.aughty.org/links.htm): an initiative that seeks to promote social integration through arts and music – long after the real integration took place.

People's natural propensity for friendship is often ignored by the political class. Instead, a more individualised and pessimistic view of human beings persists. As does the assumption that people are naturally inclined to dislike or problematise relationships with those that are 'different', rather than seeing them as opportunities to create spontaneous and potentially exciting encounters with new neighbours. This degraded and degrading thinking is in contrast to an incident in Gort in 2005. Two Brazilian men died in a fire that destroyed their house and left their families homeless. In response the local community of Gort collected enough money to contribute to the purchase of a new house for each of the families (Bilingual Community Newsletter 2006). This demonstration of empathy, of a spontaneous sense of compassion, cooperation, understanding and community, transcends the divisive notion of disparate identities promoted by governments. Gort stands as a testament to the fact that when communities are left to manage their own affairs, what we have in common often tends to count for more than the differences. The strongest message from Gort is that, far from needing authorities to mediate their relationships with the immigrant community, they were best left to their own devices. It is the politicians, as the residents of Gort might relate, that tell us we cannot cope with integration; our own experience says differently.

REFERENCES

BBC News (2004) 'Ireland votes to end birth right', *BBC News*, 13 June, http://news.bbc.co.uk/2/hi/europe/3801839.stm/ (accessed 30 April 2008)

Bilingual Community Newsletter/Jornal Bilingue da Comunidade (2006), Issue 1, February, p. 4

'Brasilian Festival in Gort, Co. Galway' (2006) blog, 7 May, http://brasilianfestivalgort.blogspot.com/ (accessed 30 April 2008)

Department of Justice, Equality and Law Reform (2005) *Planning for Diversity: The National Action Plan Against Racism*, Dublin

Fottrell, S. (2007) 'Ireland's new multicultural mix', *BBC News*, 18 May, http://news.bbc.co.uk/1/hi/world/europe/6646223.stm (accessed 30 April 2008)

Hoskins, P. (2006) 'Brazilians put new swing into small Irish town', 26 September, www.ezilon.com/information/article_16977.shtml (accessed 30 April 2008)

Irish Times (2007a) 'A Galway home for many but rough for new arrivals', 11 April

Irish Times (2007b) 'Others integration models provide options for Ireland', 20 June

Mac Cormaic, R. (2007) 'Faraway fields give Vila Gort new gloss', *Irish Times*, 11 April

Milly, J. (2003) 'Ireland tackles refugee influx', *CNN In Depth Specials*, www.cnn.com/SPECIALS/2001/immigration/stories/ireland/ (accessed 30 April 2008)

Myers, K. (2007) 'The problem isn't racism, it's the tidal wave of immigrants', *Independent* (Ireland), 5 September

Part IV

Undermining Communities

12
Communities on the Couch

Martin Earnshaw

When Frank Field wrote his 2003 book, subtitled *The Politics of Behaviour*, the kind of politics he had in mind concerned the behaviour of anti-social youths, usually living on poor housing estates. Today, however, in the space of a few years, the politics of behaviour has expanded into every sphere of life. Any form of conduct can now come under scrutiny, from binge drinking to unethical shopping. Such scrutiny is not confined to an anti-social minority, but can potentially encompass all members of society. Take the issue of binge drinking. The spectre of excessive drinking might conjure up images of unruly youths drinking cheap alcohol, therefore fitting into the dominant image of anti-social behaviour. However, it is not as straightforward as this. Elizabeth Burney (2005: 39–40) points out that until 2004 binge drinking had largely been omitted from the anti-social behaviour canon because most drinkers do not necessarily fit the stereotype of council estate-dwelling youths, but are representative of a much larger cultural phenomenon. Burney argues that it would have diluted the message about an anti-social minority 'if it were to be acknowledged that routine mass misbehaviour was an equally serious matter' (Burney 2005: 39).

The example of binge drinking represents the mainstreaming of the politics of behaviour in more ways than one. Drinking is an issue to which any concern can be attached. So as well as a problem of public order, it can also be latched onto as a symbol of moral decline, as with the hand-wringing over young women getting drunk, or as a health issue. Middle England reacted with horror when, in June 2007, the government announced that they were going to tackle the excessive drinking of wine lovers at home (Berry and Flemming 2007). Binge drinking had rapidly transmuted from a problem of anti-social behaviour to one that queried the private choices of individuals.

This blurring of the distinctions between behaviour as a public problem (i.e. anti-social) and behaviour as a private problem is evident in other discussions too. The much publicised ban on smoking in public places was presented as a response to a public health problem, the perceived effect of passive smoking. However, the ban was also designed to encourage current smokers to quit (Department of Health 2004: Ch 4: 73).

So what motivates this desire to regulate our choices? The philosopher Richard Reeves suggests that the politics of behaviour change represents a transformation in the relationship between the state and the citizen (Reeves 2008). Politicians, he believes, 'are struggling with the failure of liberal democracy to cope with issues that in the end come down to the individual'. Unhealthy eating, for example, is in liberal terms beyond the legitimate reach of the state because the resulting obesity only affects the individual. Terms like 'obesity epidemic' are therefore nonsensical.

Despite these insights, Reeves equivocates on the issue of whether the state should intervene in personal choices.

His concern is mostly about the hyperbolic language used around the issue, and the muddled thinking about policy that it engenders. He is frustrated with the government's inability to grasp the nettle of how far it should intervene and argues that the state should either intervene decisively, like slapping a tax on junk food, or back off altogether. In other words it should decide whether to be paternalistic or liberal.

Reeves's ambivalence towards state paternalism is perhaps explained by his status as an advocate of the politics of happiness. Cultivating happiness is currently a popular choice among philosophers, commentators and politicians as a goal for policy makers. Reeves has stated that politicians should take seriously people's sense of their own wellbeing and consequently the wellbeing of society as a whole (Sutherland 2008). However, if the aim of politics is to cultivate people's feeling of wellbeing, a subjective not an objective state, then the state logically cannot be anything but paternalistic.

I want to argue that the politics of wellbeing inevitably leads to the politics of behaviour. This is because it is part of a view of the role of government that leads to interference in the personal lives of citizens. Furthermore, it is typically the most socio-economically disadvantaged who are most susceptible to this control.

The politics of happiness is a public manifestation of the rise of therapeutic intervention by the state. These interventions occur where the relationship between the state (and professional agencies) and the private individual is direct and unmediated. In modern society, the relationship between the individual and the state was moderated by the public sphere: social clubs, political movements, voluntary organisations, etc. As public life has deteriorated, the state has had to find ways of gleaning information about society and acting on that information that are more individualised. The increasing reliance on psychology, opinion polls and surveys to form policy is an example of this (Furedi 2004: 61–2).

The rise of the politics of wellbeing is often attributed to affluence. Richard Layard notes that despite an unprecedented rise in wealth in the west, people are no happier. However, it is unlikely that Layard is interested in the wellbeing of city bankers; one of the main arguments of his book, *Happiness: Lessons from a New Science* (2005), is that inequality is a major cause of unhappiness.

The politics of happiness has some of its roots in studies into the psychological effects of poverty. It was not the left but the Thatcher government that first offered counselling to workers made redundant by deindustrialisation (Furedi 2004: 63). Nonetheless, the idea that relative deprivation has negative psychological effects is a key plank of New Labour's policy.

In 1996, Richard G. Wilkinson argued that the disparities in life expectancy between rich and poor were due to the increased psychological stress brought on by inequality. Wilkinson's argument was something of a breakthrough. Ever since the 1980s Black Report it had been known that inequalities in income led to unequal health and life expectancy. However, there was dispute about the cause of this. The left blamed absolute poverty; as late as 1999 it was possible for the traditional left to argue that 'poverty really is a problem of a lack of enough money – if you give people enough money, they stop being poor – it's as simple as that' (Shaw, Dorling and Davey Smith 1999: 184). This was an ineffective argument, given that overall wealth across society tends to rise, and the Conservative government took an approach that blamed poor lifestyles for the disparity in health (Fitzpatrick 2001: 75–8). The strength of Wilkinson's argument is that it takes account of the fact that inequality is relative and offers an argument for the redistribution of wealth. The problem with his argument is that by effectively redefining the problem of inequality as a psychological one, it implicitly remoralises it. The idea that deprivation psychologically damages those who experience it has the appearance of being egalitarian, as it seems to shift the blame away from poorer communities. However, it still means that those communities are subject to moral intervention.

Wilkinson's argument about inequality, as well as the moral intervention it implies, forms an important part of New Labour's policy towards social exclusion. It marks a significant shift in the perceived role of the state from redistribution with no strings attached to tacking inequality in a moral interventionist way (Levitas 2005: 112). Social exclusion covers a wide range of concerns: anti-social behaviour, health inequalities and housing. This is not a general moral condemnation of an underclass, but rather a framework for intervention into the lives of individuals. The key difference is that the socially excluded are redefined as vulnerable and then made subject to often individualised intervention.

While it may seem obvious that the poorest members of society are vulnerable, this is in fact an important change in the relationship between the state and the individual. Geoff Dench, Kate Gavron and Michael Young (2006) note that in the immediate post-war period, what was then known as the working class had a relationship with the (welfare) state that was underpinned by a mutualist model of society that was essentially contractual (Dench, Gavron and Young 2006: 215). While it is true that today the welfare state is redefined along contractual lines, the contract in the post-war period was effectively a contract with a class, not individuals. The welfare state was, in part, understood as being earned by the working class in return for their sacrifices during the Second World War. The slogan 'Home Fit for Heroes', which is commonly thought to have promoted the building of council houses, was actually coined during the First World War (Hanley 2007: 50), but it is not without reason that it is sometimes thought to have been coined after the Second.

This sense that there is a working-class community, however romanticised, which is a coherent constituency in its own right is now gone, replaced by the idea that such communities are fractured (Watts *et al.* 2008). Within such localities are not self-reliant communities, but atomised and vulnerable individuals unable to cope with the life that faces them.

A popular image of the vulnerable in such a fractured community is the one conjured up by Frank Field in *Neighbours from Hell*, of poor pensioners being besieged by anti-social yobs. However, the perpetrators of anti-social behaviour are generally seen as vulnerable too. The *Respect Action Plan* notes that '[poor] mental health, alcohol and drug problems … poor basic and life skills' are typical of the worst anti-social families (Home Office 2006: 21). Given this plethora of problems, these families are liable for intervention that extends beyond ASBOs. The Family Intervention Projects aim to assist 1,500 families a year in dealing with their problems, including teaching them how to wash and feed their children. Sometimes this takes place in specialised residential units, what some have labelled 'sin bins' (Travis 2008). If help is refused, sanctions can be imposed such as the removal of the children.

While there may be families that are dysfunctional, the number of families being talked about is worrying. The scheme also has an air of soft paternalism about it. If help is refused, the sanctions are brought into play. A final problem is that it fits into a tendency to label entire communities as basket cases. For example, Iain Duncan Smith characterises life in Britain's most deprived communities as 'dependency, addiction, debt and family breakdown' (Duncan Smith 2007). Tellingly, he approvingly quotes a Glasgow social worker who says that the 'Inner city is not a place, rather a state of mind'. Such a view is not confined to politicians. Lynsey Hanley, who grew up on a council estate, talks about the 'wall in the head' that such an upbringing creates (2007: 149). The most disadvantaged are seen as not simply limited by material poverty or physical limitations, however, but by psychological inadequacies.

If living in a deprived area psychologically disadvantages people, then this justifies pre-emptive intervention. For example, the IPPR report *Make Me a Criminal* made the case for 'a more therapeutic and family based' approach to youth offending to replace the current strategy (Margo and Stevens 2008: 3). The punitive approach to offending is not only inhumane, according to the report, but closes the door after the horse has bolted. The report puts the emphasis on early intervention before children go down the road to criminality. Among these interventions are cognitive behavioural therapy 'to address impulsiveness and other personality traits that lead to criminal activity' to be offered to disadvantaged children aged from five to twelve (Margo and Stevens 2008: 8). Like the Nurse and Family Partnership Programme (dubbed fetal ASBOs) unveiled in 2007, this is targeted at the disadvantaged as defined by area. Such early interventions are defended on the grounds that the risk of stigmatising children as potential criminals is offset by the benefits. This assumes that professionals know better than parents, but experts are as prone to prejudice as anyone else. The IPPR report advocates the banning of smacking on the grounds that it would not only reduce crime, but to 'send out a signal about the kind of society we want to be' (Margo and Stevens 2008: 6). This 'evidence based' position is naive in the extreme and indicates that experts should not necessarily be treated with uncritical deference. Indeed expert knowledge often upholds an ideological view of child-rearing free from the messiness of the real world, both promoting an intensive mother–child relationship isolated from wider society and the indispensability of expert knowledge without which day-to-day parenting is impossible (Hays 1996: 64).

It may be objected that, given the advanced state of decay within some communities, only the state can provide the glue for socialisation to happen. This view is the one that primarily informs the *Respect Action Plan*. In his foreword Tony Blair stated that it was not in the remit of central government to re-establish norms of behaviour, only local communities could do that, but government could provide a broad framework of legal powers and other approaches through which to promote good behaviour and crack down on anti-social behaviour (Home Office 2006: 1). Elsewhere the plan says that tackling anti-social behaviour will make communities more confident, and 'where people feel confident, safe and supported, they will be able to come together with others in their neighbourhood to build trust, share values and agree what is acceptable behaviour' (Home Office 2006: 3). So the idea is that if the state intervenes now, this will provide the framework for neighbourhoods to establish norms of behaviour spontaneously later. A key factor in this is the building up of confidence and trust. However, the danger is that intervention denies the space necessary for the relations of trust to develop that social bonds depend upon.

In the case of parenting, the intervention of experts into the parent–child relationship feeds into the commonplace view that parents are mainly abusive and feckless, a position commonly articulated as 'I blame the parents'; but if this is how parents are seen, why should children respect them? As for the responsibility for wider society to socialise children, all adults who volunteer for any activity involving children are required to be vetted under the 2006 Safeguarding Vulnerable Groups Act. Volunteering is a valuable socialising activity, but such regulations and the prevailing sense of mistrust they feed off may deter people who would otherwise come forward. Since state intervention is often predicated on the assumption that people can't be trusted, it cannot build bonds.

What of the *Respect Action Plan*'s claim that tackling anti-social behaviour will help build the confidence and trust, and hence community? What is interesting about the crusade against anti-social behaviour is that it essentially constitutes a form of therapy. Although the British Crime Survey has consistently shown that nationally overall crime rates are far lower than the 1995 peak, perception that crime is out of control is still prevalent. Government policy is aimed, not so much to decrease crime, but to decrease this feeling of unease (Home Office 2003, 2007).

Anti-social behaviour fits into this framework because almost anything can fall into the category. The ASBO was inspired by the civil injunctions imposed in the USA to combat disorder. However, Burney (2005: 2) notes that anti-social behaviour is a fundamentally different thing from disorder or incivilities. Whereas disorder is a problem affecting neighbour-hoods, anti-social *behaviour* refers primarily to the individual.

This is reflected in the ASBO itself, which is personalised for the individual to which it is given. It has been often noted that the well-publicised cases of youths with ASBOs being unable to enter certain streets and locations are an easy way for the state to keep tabs on potential troublemakers, but they are also tailored towards anything that the public feels uneasy towards.

The point that is missed is that the very act of trying to reassure the public actually increases the sense that the neighbourhood is a dangerous place (Burney 2005: 10–12). Not only does this undermine the self-reliance of individuals and communities, it can also lead to a perception that communities are unable to be self-reliant. The idea that the state has a responsibility for dealing with minor problems that would have been dealt with by members of the public themselves becomes institutionalised. People instinctively reach for the phone rather than talk to their neighbours (Burney 2005: 80–1).

We began this chapter by surveying the spread of the politics of behaviour. Richard Reeves correctly noted that such politics presents a challenge to the liberal state. However, we have sought to show that the relationship between the state and the citizen is fundamentally different than in the past. In answer to Reeves's criticism of the term 'obesity epidemic' for example, it could be argued that obesity disproportionately affects the poor, and obesity can thus be described as a social pathology just like social exclusion and anti-social behaviour. These are now the terms on which the state manages social problems. A relationship that is essentially therapeutic casts individuals as passive vessels onto which the state can project its interventions.

Ostensibly, this is intended to rebuild society through creating frameworks through which communities can flourish.

However, this approach is in danger of creating a dependency, since individuals are deemed incapable of taking responsibility for themselves and their communities into their own hands. Although this problem is most keenly felt in the most deprived neighbourhoods, the fact that society at large is accepting of petty bans and a public discussion that problematises lifestyle suggests that the passive attitude to the state is more widespread than this. Terms such as 'soft paternalism' (Reeves 2008) and 'pro-social behaviour' (Taylor 2007) describe attempts to manipulate public behaviour though incentives and sanctions derived from psychology. If this is not quite infantalisation, it creates, as a 2007 MORI poll puts it, a relationship between the state and the public that is akin to a step-parent–teenager relationship (Page 2007). The poll also, however, found that citizens were ambivalent about this process: paradoxically, 61 per cent of respondents thought that governments should ban dangerous activities while 62 per cent thought that the government didn't trust people to make their own decisions. This apparent ambivalence shouldn't be taken as anti-statism, in fact it is an indication of individuation (the poll also found that respondents see themselves as customers of the state). However, if people have the basic self-respect to make their own decisions it may form the limits to the moral activist state.

REFERENCES

Berry, A. and Flemming, N. (2007) 'Wine lovers targeted to cut binge drinking', *Daily Telegraph*, 6 June

Burney, E. (2005) *Making People Behave: Anti-social Behaviour, Politics and Policy* Devon, Willan Publishing

Dench, G., Gavron, K. and Young, M. (2006) *The New East End*, London, Profile Books Ltd

Department of Health (2004) *Choosing Health: Making Choices Easier*, White Paper

Duncan Smith, I. (2007) 'Can our broken society by fixed?', *Daily Telegraph*, 8 July

Hanley, L. (2007) *Estates: An Intimate History*, London, Granta

Field, F. (2003) *Neighbours from Hell: The Politics of Behaviour*, London, Politicos

Fitzpatrick, M. (2001) *The Tyranny of Health*, London, Routledge

Furedi, F. (2004) *Therapy Culture: Cultivating Vulnerability in an Uncertain Age*, London, Routledge

Hays, S. (1996) *The Cultural Contradictions of Mother-hood*, London, Yale University Press

Home Office (2003) 'Crime in England and Wales 2002/2003', Home Office Statistical Bulletin, ed. Jon Simmons and Tricia Dodd, July, pp. 2–3

Home Office (2006) *Respect Action Plan*, 10 January, see also www. respect.gov.uk (accessed 29 June 2008)

Home Office (2007) 'Crime in England and Wales 2006/2007', Home Office Statistical Bulletin, ed. Sian Nicholas, Chris Kershaw and Alison Walker, July, p. 18

Layard, R. (2005), *Happiness: Lessons from a New Science*, London, Penguin

Levitas, R. (2005) *The Inclusive Society: Social Exclusion and New Labour* (2nd edition), London, Palgrave Macmillan

Margo, J. and Stevens, A. (02.2008) *Make Me a Criminal: Preventing Youth Crime*, London, Institute for Public Policy Research (IPPR)

Page, B. (2007) 'Citizens have their say', Mori research for HM Policy Review, January, http://archive.cabinetoffice.gov.uk/policy_review/public_engagement/index.asp (accessed 29 June 2008)

Reeves, R. (2008) 'The naughty nation', *New Statesman*, 14 February

Shaw, M., Dorling, D. and Davey Smith, G. (1999) *The Widening Gap*, Bristol, Policy Press

Sutherland, J. (2008) 'The ideas interview: Richard Reeves', *Guardian*, 30 May

Taylor, M. (2007) 'Pro-social behaviour – the future: it's up to us', Royal Society of Arts (RSA lecture), 7 February, www.rsa.org.uk/acrobat/pro-social_behaviour.pdf (accessed 29 April 2008)

Travis, A. (2008) 'Sin bin scheme for 1,500 families a year', *Guardian*, 12 April

Watts, B., Lloyd, C., Mowlam, A. and Creegan, C. (2008) *What Are Today's Social Evils?*, Joseph Rowntree Foundation, April

Wilkinson, R. (1996) *Unhealthy Societies: The Afflictions of Inequality*, London, Routledge

13
Youthful Misbehaviour or Adult Traumas?

Stuart Waiton

Recently, the discussion about anti-social behaviour has at times moved beyond the 'yob culture' rant and raised some concern about the declining number of adults who are prepared to 'have a go' when faced with misbehaving youngsters. This occasional move to discuss not just what young people are up to but what adults are doing is a welcome addition to the ASBO debate.

This chapter will argue that a, and arguably *the*, major problem regarding adult–youth relations is not the activities of youth but the inactivity of adults: inactivity that has emerged in part because of the growing regulation of everyday life.

Without accepted norms of engagement predicated upon a certain level of freedom and trust, adults today often feel paralysed, unsure of themselves and of their role in either regulating the behaviour of young people or simply supporting children they encounter in their daily lives. Instead of an accepted framework for relating to children and young people that is grounded in lived experiences established by an active public, today an ersatz form of socialisation is taking hold, which leaves both adults and young people increasingly disconnected from one another.

The socialising role of publicly acting adults is crucial for any society. Unfortunately, as this chapter will attempt to show, much of the social policy being developed apparently to socialise young people is in essence based upon an approach that can best be described as one that results in the *anti-socialisation* of society.

DANGEROUS YOUTH?

The lack of active adults who are prepared to intervene when young people misbehave was noted in 2006 by the Institute for Public Policy Research (IPPR). In a paper entitled *Freedom's Orphans*, the IPPR observed that whereas in Germany two-thirds of adults said they would intervene if they saw a group of young people vandalising a bus shelter, in the UK only a third of adults surveyed said they would act (Margo and Dixon 2006).

A key reason for this development, argued the IPPR, was the fear that adults had of young people. As they argued, 'Britain is in danger of becoming a nation fearful of its young people'. In a YouGov opinion poll it was similarly found that 42 per cent of adults did not feel safe in the neighbourhood at night, largely because of the behaviour of youngsters.

Implicit within the discussion concerning adult fears about young people is the idea that somehow today's teenagers are genuinely dangerous and a threat to adults in the UK. But, despite extreme examples such as the murder of Gary Newlove – a man who attempted to intervene when three young men were vandalising a car in his street – are we really, as these surveys suggest, at risk from teenagers?

Would these adults feel so anxious if they thought that by intervening in the behaviour of young people, they would be supported by the young people's parents, and backed up by other adults in their neighbourhood? Indeed, if instead of one-third of adults being prepared to act, two-thirds or more did so, would Gary Newlove be alive today?

It may be unfair and illegitimate to isolate one extreme example like this, but adult solidarity is key to understanding the problem of (and the *problematisation* of) youth behaviour, and more broadly to any understanding of the socialisation of children and young people.

A QUESTION OF TRUST

Cases such as the Newlove murder are to some extent distracting. Most of us do not live next to 'neighbours from hell', or come across young 'terrorists', as Labour MP Frank Field calls them (Field 2003). But the question of youth misbehaviour should not simply be dismissed as a moral panic. All of us I suspect have at one time or another come across young people misbehaving, dropping litter, swearing or vandalising property, and most of us appear to feel afraid, or at least unsure about intervening and saying something to these young people.

In 2001, I wrote a book entitled *Scared of the Kids?*, which, while focusing on the introduction of one of the first curfew initiatives in the UK, also examined more broadly the reasons why adults felt so anxious about young people. Fear or at least a sense of unease about young people was already well established at this time, and my research then as now was to understand the social causes of this development. Sifting through a variety of documents at the time, it was interesting that one of the most perceptive comments I came across was not in any government paper, or to be found in the variety of think tank research publications on the topic, but in the letters page of a local Glasgow newspaper. Here, an ex-teacher of 30 years explained:

> As a parent and grandparent I endorse the policy which dictates: No talking to strangers ... accepting lifts in cars ... walking by yourself in parks or isolated places! But we seem near a point where children are programmed to TRUST no one. The result is that many well intentioned adults are terrified of being seen trying to make contact with children. Is it any wonder the generation gap widens by the minute? (*Evening Times*, 15 January 1997)

The letter, entitled 'My Shame Over Lack of Courage', it was written by ex-teacher Catherine McGuiness. She explained how she had walked past a group of teenagers who were dropping litter in the park, and had said nothing.

McGuiness said that approaching children was for many adults more difficult because children had been 'programmed to trust no one', rather than simply because of their anti-social behaviour. On her part she felt she had 'chickened out' of challenging these young people. She asked herself whether she had 'joined the adults who have opted out of civic responsibility'. She wondered, '[h]ave adults become so frightened of the younger generation they're prepared to look the other way rather than tangle with them?' (Waiton 2001: 133).

This example is particularly useful because it illustrates the interconnection between a declining sense of surety about the rules of engagement when dealing with young people, and the subsequent paralysis of someone who had spent their life *dealing* with young people.

Today the lack of assurance felt by adults can be witnessed daily in almost any situation where there are children. Boarding an aeroplane last year, I witnessed an embarrassed mother and father attempt to round up their three small children. Each insisted upon running away as soon as one of their hands was released by the exasperated parents. The staff and 150 passengers squirmed in their seats and clearly sympathised with the parents, and yet none of them felt able to offer the mother and father any assistance.

Understanding the fear of intervening, or even engaging children and young people, is not simply about the problematic nature of today's youth. It is perhaps more usefully understood, in this context, as something to do with the confused relationship that now exists between adults and other people's children.

DEACTIVATING ADULTS

The myopic focus on anti-social behaviour allows what is a question for society at large – of civic responsibility, trust and solidarity between adults – to be reduced to a question of violent youth and marginalised families. The issue of collective public norms regarding how we behave towards children is consequently avoided – either through an individuated focus on the family, or by discussing the need for more and better professional support, mentoring and policing of young people. Ultimately today, the question of socialisation and the role that the public plays in the process of socialising other people's children is sidestepped.

One of my concerns in writing *Scared of the Kids* was that curfews and anti-social behaviour initiatives would lead to a situation whereby local adults, who were already unsure about their role with regards young people, would be further discouraged from becoming active in their communities. In the area where I live, CCTV cameras have recently been introduced. In protest, I wrote a leaflet making the following points:

> Some people have said to me that they aren't that keen on the cameras – but, 'what harm can they do?' For me, the biggest problem of all ... is that it encourages adults to be more afraid of young people and to play a less active role in their own community ... for many adults living here it will only confirm their suspicions about the dangerous nature of the young people of the area. Suspicions that are often unjustified. By introducing cameras in the area, the police and the local MP are sending out the message that it is not local adults who should regulate the behaviour of young people, but the police ... The CCTV cameras will simply reinforce this idea and discourage adults from resolving difficulties they may be having with local youngsters.

Here, like almost everywhere else in the UK, adults have been encouraged to see the regulation of young people as the job of the police and professionals. Indeed it would be interesting to know if people still feel a sense of shame at their own inaction today, as Catherine McGuiness did ten years ago; or whether instead their passivity has been insti-tutionalised and justified by the routine involvement of the growing array of community wardens, police officers and professional surveillance, which has come to occupy what was once *public* space.

ANTI-SOCIAL

While paying lip service to the idea of community, the move towards regulating spontaneous relationships between people has developed apace in the last decade, as the politics of behaviour has filtered its way down into the micro-management of everyday life.

For example, the left-leaning IPPR, addressing what they describe in their report *Freedom's Orphans* as the 'socialisation gap', discuss the issue of socialising young people with little reference to the public. Indeed, their recommendations with regards to the 'state of youth' steer clear of any notion that young people should be socialised by local adults, their peer group or by society more generally. The authors, Julia Margo and Mike Dixon, think that the job of socialising the young should be performed by paid professionals engaging them in regulated 'positive' activities. Break up traditional hierarchies and peer groups in schools, they advise, and train teachers to improve the personal and social skills of their pupils.

The informal sphere where relationships between adults and children can develop are a footnote in the report. Teachers' traditional role as educators able to develop the minds of young people is ignored in favour of re-skilling them to administer the latest behaviour techniques for bringing their charges under control. Similarly, the role played by young people themselves, through their peer groups, in socialising with one another, attending unstructured youth groups or just hanging about, is only understood as a problem by the IPPR authors.

A mere think tank document this may be – but the IPPR approach both reflects and informs current social policy, which is riddled with talk of structured activities, mentoring, emotional management classes and relationship education in schools. Like the development of CCTV, ASBOs and community wardens, these developments reflect an approach to life devoid of relatively free or unregulated relationships. Indeed, it is an approach that both problematises and pro-fessionalises any relationship that is not mediated by the appropriate professional, or the latest techniques developed by the most recent child expert.

Today, local football teams, after-school clubs and school discos are increasingly regulated, with vetting of staff and volunteers and myriad procedures and codes of conduct, which allow little, if any, initiative or spontaneity by those adults who are still prepared to give up their time to engage and develop young people. In many ways, young people's lives have never been so systematically *managed*. But this does not mean that they are being *socialised*, it means the reverse.

ANTI-SOCIALISATION

Today there appears to be a lot of discussion about public norms. Indeed politicians themselves have increasingly seen their role as facilitating respect in the community. However, through the ASBO debate and the promotion of a *Quiet Life* (Labour 1995) the public development of norms has largely been abandoned. Having vacated the terrain of morality and politics that can provide a basis for commonality and camaraderie between people, state institutions have colonised the space where individuals have previously developed interpersonal norms of behaviour between the generations. With the diminution of an active public, new expert norms are being developed by think tanks and paid professionals armed with the latest codes of conduct and zero tolerance initiatives.

In the process, relationships developed in the community are formalised. By professionalising previously informal areas of life – by institutionalising everything from the need for a safety certificate before you can run a kids disco, and giving medicalised labels to children who misbehave (e.g. ADHD), to encouraging the idea that rowdy youngsters should be dealt with by council officials or community support officers – the confidence of adults to trust themselves and one another, to understand and to act spontaneously towards young people, is being continually undermined.

In effect norms, as socially developed modes of behaviour, negotiated between the generations are being taken out of our hands. This applies as much to noisy neighbours and disruptive youth as it does to inconsiderate commuters using their mobiles or dropping litter (see Transport For London's 'Are You a Considerate Passenger?' campaign).

The fear that adults express in relation to young people is a reflection of a culture that no longer has an agreed framework whereby adults feel able to trust and support each other – one where we are not only unsure about how young people will react when we intervene, but are even more wary of the reactions and assumptions of other adults. We are no longer sure about other people and consequently are no longer sure of ourselves. Rather than acting spontaneously, whether in the street, in schools, youth clubs or even in the home, we are looking over our shoulder waiting to be questioned, criticised, accused or held to account by officials wielding an array of behavioural codes that are not our own.

It is perhaps easy to forget, given this cultural and political backdrop, that personal conflict is a normal part of everyday life. Unfortunately, third party intervention makes conflict resolution between people impossible, and promotes distrust in the community. A first step in overcoming this situation would be to provide people with more freedom to act for themselves, to develop their own norms and to be able to socialise the young, free from the corrosive mediations of self-appointed guardians of our communities.

REFERENCES

Field, F. (2003) *Neighbours from Hell: The Politics of Behaviour*, London, Politicos

Labour Party (1995) *A Quiet Life: Tough Action on Criminal Neighbours*, London, Labour Party

Margo, J. and Dixon, M. (2006) *Freedom's Orphans: Raising Youth in a Changing World*, London, IPPR

Waiton, S. (2001) *Scared of the Kids? Curfews, Crime and the Regulation of Young People*, Sheffield, Sheffield Hallam University Press

14
Parish Pump Politics

Dave Clements

Today, we are urged to become 'active citizens' working to improve our local communities from the bottom up, as volunteers, as residents, as school governors, even as local councillors. But central government, apparently eager to hand more power to the people, regards local authorities as unworthy representatives, more an obstacle to passing on that power to communities. What David Miliband, when he was the UK's minister for communities and local government, described as 'double devolution' (Miliband 2006) (that is, both to councils and to communities themselves), the current incumbent, Hazel Blears, describes as '[d]evolution right to the doorstep' (Blears 2007). With her self-assured and thoroughly superficial common touch, Blears declares herself to be steeped in the localist creed: 'my whole political approach, fashioned on the streets and estates of Salford, is anchored in localism and devolution', she says (Blears 2007). The leader of the opposition, David Cameron, also describes himself as a 'convinced localist' (*Guardian* 2007).

The politics of localism and devolution, however, do not reside in the personalities of senior political figures, still less in their municipal pasts. Like the insistent rhetoric of involvement and participation, the political elite is increasingly eager that we and they 'go local' too. There has been much talk recently about reforming the way government works, particularly local government, and particularly with regards the problem of engaging communities. According to the Local Government Association, 'major devolution to local government is the first building block in a much-needed renaissance of democracy and trust' (Ives 2007). The Lyons Inquiry into local government recommended that councils become 'place shapers', building public trust and confidence, through better engagement with citizens; and by freeing local authorities from the stranglehold of centrally imposed targets and inspections (Lyons 2007).

The subsequent local government White Paper, *Strong and Prosperous Communities*, was meant to indicate the government's 'confidence in local government, local communities and other local public service providers by giving them more freedom and powers to bring about the changes they want to see' (DCLG 2006). The most recent instalment of this 'ambitious devolution agenda' – another White Paper, published in the summer of 2008 – will further 'the government's ambition for local authorities to lead the way towards more active citizenship, empowered communities, and ultimately, a revival of local democracy' (LGIU 2008).

LOCAL GOVERNANCE: A CENTRAL IDEA

There is a lot of inflated rhetoric about giving individuals power and influence in their communities, most of it (the rhetoric not the power) coming from the communities minister herself. For instance, Blears talks about 'bringing government closer to people' (Blears 2007) so that we can have a say about the kinds of things that affect us. We'll discuss what sort of 'things' she has in mind in a moment, but why would the government want to bring themselves closer to communities anyway? According to a leader article in the *Guardian* after last year's Local Government Association Conference, the 'assumption is that decision-making is more legitimate, and more trustworthy, if it is done locally ... [and] that breaking things up will allow people to feel more engaged' (*Guardian* 2007).

The political commentator Polly Toynbee, also writing in the *Guardian*, is critical of what she describes as the 'sentimental localists, enthusiasts for pavement politics, [who] think local is small and cosy' and who 'vainly hope that pushing power down to communities will magically make the disaffected eager to run things at street level' (Toynbee 2007). This, she says, has 'an air of desperation, out of denial of the real problem'. Indeed, it does, but what is most striking is that it is the political centre that has so wholeheartedly embraced the local; or, at least, has sought to impose on local government its own diminished view of politics as something that is essentially local, not only in its conduct but also in its focus and scope. This is the kind of politics that gave us the petty posturing over the 'alternate weekly' rubbish collection, which dominated the local elections in 2007; and that in 2008 gave us the vexed issue of 'bendy buses' in the race to decide who would run the 'world city' of London.

But though this pavement politics is often silly and always inadequate in so many ways, its dynamic is thoroughly authoritarian. This is evident in the utterances of advocates of the New Localism. Chris Leslie, director of the New

Local Government Network, for instance, proposes 'radical' solutions to the problems that communities experience. He wants these solutions to 'emerge street by street, in the local community itself, rather than from on high ... cutting through bureaucracy that too often hampers the sort of timely and caring intervention' that communities need (Leslie 2007). The rhetoric may sound attractive and go-getting, but it is typically cavalier (not to mention patronising of communities) in its easy dismissal of those authorities 'on high' and the local bureaucracies that get in the way of the kinds of interventions he wants to see. Leslie seems to forget, or else ignores, that these institutions about which he is so disparaging are democratically accountable; and they make and administer policy not on the basis of a comment piece in the *Guardian*, but because people pay their taxes and vote for local councillors to represent them. He, on the other hand, is an unelected lobbyist. But oddly it is their legitimacy, not his, that is called into question.

FROM COUNCILLORS TO COUNSELLORS

While defending local politicians from self-appointed representatives of the community, it is nevertheless not altogether surprising that people are put off by the dustbin devolution of our emptied out managerial politics. According to surveys, and despite improving annual performance assessments (with most local authorities being rated 'good' or 'very good' by inspectors), half of councils leave their constituents feeling 'unsatisfied' (Kelly 2007). But then auditors, using the Comprehensive Performance Assessment (CPA) to evaluate the quality of local services, are unlikely to be using the same criteria as local people when it comes to judging their performance. Still, enthusiasts for local government renewal would rather blame local politicians, as well as the apathy and ignorance of local people, than interrogate the state of local politics itself. Councillors, they say, are too old, too male and too white, and that apparently makes them unrepresentative.

Modernisers seem to be convinced that the wrong sorts of people are running local government. They complain that the life of the local councillor is just too demanding, and therefore not an attractive option for the right sorts of people. So, Lucy de Groot, executive director of the government's Improvement and Development Agency, argues that potential councillors are being put off by the prospect of a heavy workload. Former communities minister, Ruth Kelly, thinks that prospective councillors with children are unable to serve their communities as a consequence of 'inadequate childcare, [and] too many late-night town hall meetings' (Wintour 2007). But instead of proposing to her colleagues in government that round-the-clock universal childcare is urgently needed if our future representatives are to achieve an acceptable work–life balance, she set up the Independent Councillors Commission (Ives 2007).

The final report of the Commission concluded that what is needed is 'a more diverse range of people to become councillors so that communities are better represented' (DCLG 2007a). Another report, *Ward Councillors and Community Leadership: A Future Perspective*, this time from the Young Foundation and Local Government Information Unit, came to the same conclusion (James and Cox 2007). By getting into local government people who are more able to engage with diverse communities, so the argument goes, the legitimacy of local politics and the health of local democracy will be renewed. But this is destined to fail. Because what is being advocated here is not better political representation for local people; but rather an attempt to find the kinds of individuals who are better able to represent the interests of a political class that feels itself to be hopelessly out of touch with the people.

Like Leslie's anti-democratic impulse to do away with the existing structures of local democracy in favour of his own version of 'direct democracy', this failure to recognise councillors' legitimacy as elected members of their local authorities brings into doubt the democratic credentials of those who seek to reform local government. It is also self-defeating for the political elite because by valorising accidents of birth, such as a councillor's age, gender or ethnicity, only the most superficial connection with an increasingly cynical public can result. Further to this, by understanding representation in this way, and by looking for councillors who are 'just like us', there is a very real risk that we will end up with counsellors instead – professional strangers with whom we engage as troubled individuals, rather than hold to account as our political representatives.

Already, local politicians seem less interested in accounting for shoddy public services, and more disposed to attending to individuated outcomes, our happiness, quality of life or psychological wellbeing. This turns what are social and political problems into personal maladies; something that is not only worryingly intrusive, but also reinforces the impression that our political leaders are unable to come up with the kinds of inspiring policy ideas, or practical solutions, that can genuinely engage people as a consequence of improving the lot of communities.

THE LOCAL GETS PERSONAL

Instead it is public service innovations like 'devolved or
delegated budgets' (Ministry of Justice 2007) and 'participatory
budgeting' (Bullard 2007) with which communities are to be
enthused. The latter is a scheme modelled on Porto Alegre in
Brazil where 'some of the world's most deprived people' get 'a
direct say in how money is spent', according to Blears (2007).
People in the UK too, says the communities minister excitedly,
'will be able to decide whether their priority is play areas,
youth facilities, traffic calming or more community wardens'.
(It also helps with the government's determination to cut
spending on public services.) As if to confirm the therapeutic-
turn in the way local government relates to communities,
one of the local authorities piloting participatory budgeting
explained that 'having been involved in the decision making,
people feel better about themselves and their community'
(Bullard 2007).

The message seems to be that although there won't be any
more money available, and although you will be given the
responsibility for deciding whether the playground or the
speed humps get the go-ahead, at least you will feel better
about it. This coercive responsibilising character of the
community agenda, and the logical endpoint in the localising
of responsibility, is particularly evident in the personalising
of ostensibly public services. As cabinet office minister Ed
Miliband described it recently:

> We need more personal services – that means being centred [on] the
> user, but also being more personal to the user in the sense of being
> tailored to their individual needs. Secondly, responsive public services
> is not just about delivering to people, but also what the individual can
> contribute ... We need parents to contribute to their kids' education

and for people with chronic conditions to help manage them, possibly using individual budgets. (Wintour 2008)

Charles Leadbeater at Demos is particularly excited by the potential of personal budgets to transform service users into 'participants' in the delivery of services, or in their own care management. Yet, while this might for some be a welcome shift from dependency on inadequate services, it is hard to see the advantage for the most vulnerable, or for those simply with better things to do with their time. But then individual budgets have not only been shown to cut costs for hard-up local authorities, as Leadbeater enthusiastically acknowledges, but they also have the potential to nurture the kind of relationship between the individual and the state that the government wants to encourage. Leadbeater describes those who administer their own care, or who commission their own services, as typically 'optimistic, energetic and confident' (Leadbeater 2008). They are no longer just passively receiving services, but instead exhibiting the kind of character traits conducive to becoming an 'active citizen'.

THE PETTY POLITICS OF THE PARISH

However, this is an impoverished notion of citizenship that is in keeping only with the political elite's diminished view of ordinary people and what they should aspire to. Blears argues that doing politics the local way is 'the only way we can get to grips with some of the biggest challenges we face – from climate change to childhood obesity – where people making little changes in their everyday life is a vital part of the solution' (Blears 2007). It is this preference for 'little changes' that sums up the low horizons and patronising assumptions of our political leaders, and continues to ensure that even the 'biggest challenges' we face must be reduced to the lifestyle politics of fat kids and green wheelie bins.

So, when 'radical proposals to make people's voices heard on the key issues they care most about' (the much heralded 'petition powers') were announced, it was not surprising to find that those proposals were anything but 'radical'; and that the 'key issues' as far as the government were concerned were parochial, timid ones, 'such as tackling anti-social behaviour, helping older people or improving local parks ... from abandoned vehicles to youth services' (DCLG 2007b). These are also the sorts of issues that are designed to indulge people's worries and anxieties about scary youths and neighbourhood decline, health epidemics and environmental collapse.

CONCLUSION

The items on the localist agenda are not only doom-laden, but represent a doomed attempt at building a sense of community through a shared culture of fear. This reflects a devolution discourse that has turned what is a political problem for a disoriented elite into an opportunity for the further undermining of local representatives' capacity to effect change on communities' behalves.

Indeed, old-style council chamber politics – the very stuff of real democracy, however moribund – is regarded as an obstacle to be overcome, like the bureaucracy of local government itself, better to get at communities. At the same time, however, as the authorities seek to engage with communities and devolve power (or at least offload responsibilities) to them, there is an instinctive withdrawal from the public at the level of politics.

This is why the localist idea is so demeaning of the very notion of people having a say over the substantive matters that affect them. It is indicative of the reduction of politics to the insubstantive or, to paraphrase Toynbee, to the pedestrian politics of the pavement. The tyranny of the local is the enemy of the imagination. It reduces everything, to put it another way, to the petty politics of the parish. The local is too narrow a terrain for meaningful interventions in the political sphere, and consequently limited in its capacity to enhance the wellbeing of communities, even if this ostensible goal had any reality to it. Like the rise of the politics of behaviour, the retreat to the local expresses well the parochialising of public life. We should instead be initiating a genuinely unbounded dialogue, uninhibited by the parochial and the fearful obsessions of which we are all too familiar, about how communities can realise their collective interests, address the problems they share and move on to bigger things.

REFERENCES

Blears, H. (2007) 'Confident communities', speech to Development Trusts Association Annual Conference at Oxford Town Hall, 17 September

Bullard, R. (2007) 'More hands on the purse strings', *Guardian*, 4 April

DCLG (2006) *Strong and Prosperous Communities: The Local Government White Paper*

DCLG (2007a) *Representing the future: The report of the Councillors Commission*, 14 March

DCLG (2007b) 'Petition power kicks off new year of community action', press release, 27 December

Guardian (2007) 'Local difficulties', leader article, 6 June

Ives, J. (2007) 'Heavy workload "deterring would-be councillors"' *Society Guardian*, 14 March

James, S. and Cox, E. (2007) *Ward Councillors and Community Leadership: A Future Perspective*, a study for the Joseph Rowntree Foundation by the Young Foundation and LGiU

Kelly, A. (2007) 'Councils can give no satisfaction', *Guardian*, 27 June

Leadbeater, C. (2008) 'This time it's personal', *Guardian*, 16 January

Leslie, C. (2007) 'Breaking boundaries', *Society Guardian*, 19 April

Local Government Information Unit (2008) 'Power to the people: will the White Paper deliver?' conference at Congress Centre in London, 15 May

Lyons, M. (2007) 'Place-shaping: a shared ambition for the future of local government', Stationery Office

Miliband, D. (2006) Keynote speech to National Council for Voluntary Organisations (NCVO), annual conference, 21 February, www.ncvo-vol.org.uk/events/speeches/?id=2382/ (accessed 5 July 2008)

Ministry of Justice (2007) *The Governance of Britain* (Green Paper)

Toynbee, P. (2007) 'This vogue for localism has not solved voter antipathy', *Guardian*, 8 May

Wintour, P. (2007) 'Kelly's £10,000 idea to attract councillors', *Guardian*, 9 February

Wintour, P. (2008) 'Miliband: No turning back on reform of public services', *Guardian*, 7 February

Conclusion:
A Death Greatly Exaggerated

Alastair Donald

Unruly toddlers, hoodies with handguns, anti-social behaviour and alcohol-fuelled disorder, blighted estates. All common visions of a broken, anarchic Britain. For those who take a bleak view of the future for communities, all of these were applied to the brutal killing in Croxteth, Liverpool, of eleven-year-old Rhys Jones in the summer of 2007. After Conservative leader David Cameron had asserted the need to realise a culture change that could offset an alleged descent into 'anarchy in the UK' (Cameron 2007), his posturing sound-bite was regurgitated as the despairing banner headline for the recriminations and soul searching that followed.

Ironically, when the Sex Pistols marketed their own anarchic brand of nihilistic individualism 30 years ago, it signalled the death throes of the post-war consensus. Then, opting out became visibly more appealing than the staid institutions of collective identity. However, today, appropriated by politicians, leader writers and newspaper columnists, 'Anarchy in the UK' no longer represents a youthful two fingers to society's leaders, but is the sentiment that captures the outlook and fears of the leaders and opinion formers themselves. Fearful of communities with whom they have little empathy or relationship; unable to inspire commitment or even provide a sense of purpose in society; in their exaggerated sense of dislocation, it is those leading society who now appear to subscribe to the notion of No Future.

It is this nexus of community and society that has been addressed in this book. On the one hand, we have investigated the localised form in which the breakdown in society is experienced and in which the debates about the future are played out; on the other, we have looked at the broader political and social context that is largely neglected in the communities' debate, but which, as the chapters illustrate, ultimately underpin the shape, direction and experience of this breakdown. In this sense we can conclude that the discussion on the future of community is not really about community at all. It is first and foremost a debate about the nature and future of society, albeit one in which the key dimensions are rarely drawn out and treated as such. The task we set for our writers was to uncover the real meaning of the debates on community. The wide-ranging nature of the material in their responses capture the manner in which, transposed from society to community, the contemporary debate on the future is not always an obvious one.

The common response to high-profile crime incidents such as the murder of Rhys Jones or the kidnapping of Sharon Matthews is for newspaper editors and think tank directors to dispatch their correspondents and researchers to far flung areas of the UK to find out just how it is that the 'natives' live. Such a response is indicative of deep uncertainty of those at the head of contemporary society. Take for example the furore which broke out after home secretary Jacqui Smith admitted to the *Sunday Times* that she was scared of being out on the streets of London at night – something millions of us routinely negotiate on a daily basis. To offset the resulting bad publicity her press office made it known that she had in fact recently been for a kebab in Peckham, the area of inner south London that is discussed almost entirely in terms of its murder rate. Accompanied by her security guards, Smith reportedly asked the kebab shop owner, 'What's it like round here?' as if stranded in a foreign land.

This level of incomprehension not only creates an impetus for exaggerating the sense of communities out of control, but also helps explain the barrage of focus groups, consultation initiatives and engagement exercises which we are urged to become involved in and which appear to fill the lives of a generation of politician managers. Many commentators take at face value the assertions that these represent attempts to create new forms of democratic politics. Yet it is clear that what Dave Clements in his chapter in this book refers to as the 'participatory paradigm' is actually an attempt to locate the public, and to fix some points of connection with it. Once a line of communication is established, the new ethos of localist participation means that engaging communities in service delivery, developing community responsibilities and boosting self-esteem are all to the fore. Yet all these initiatives seem designed to offset the organising authority's own perception of instability; they are procedural measures for formalising the connection and then managing community affairs.

It seems that participation initiatives are less the means to reviving local democracy and politics, than a substitute. This book indicates that in order to reclaim the notion of having a genuine stake in collectively shaping our lives, it is important to reject the culture of manage, measure, audit, and the array of new institutional arrangements that serve to formalise the relations between individuals and increasingly to bureaucratise community life. There is absolutely nothing positive about having the right to manage the delivery of community services; there are, however, many genuine concerns that the restricted freedoms which result from these arrangements will undermine the ability of communities to act as independent citizens and autonomous individuals.

A number of our contributors have laid bare the paternalistic assumptions that inform the idea that communities need to be created by external forces. One consequence that comes through time and again is the rise of a vast industry of 'community creators' who now exist both within and without officialdom. The time and effort spent bringing the public into new forums and consultation processes – which translates as drawing them into official relationships through which external influences can be brought to bear on the shape and actions of local communities – is symptomatic of the lack of trust authorities have for the public, and their low regard for the notion of a voluntaristic public life.

Although they are far from alone, in particular we have highlighted the role of the design and planning professions at the forefront of this insidious trend. Far too often these professions accept the official line that the design of buildings or public spaces have been responsible for the breakdown of community, and that the right spaces or better community engagement processes can tune behaviour in a way that fosters community revival. It is often the interventions of designers, planners – and a myriad of other professions one step removed from authority – that lead the charge in terms of social engineering exercises which, whether intended or otherwise, have the effect of interfering in individual choices. By providing a conduit for official interventions into community life, these initiatives clearly have the effect of further estranging communities from the idea that they have an independent capacity to organise themselves to determine the shape of their communities. It's about time that professionals who work with communities examined their role and got on with delivering the services that they are there to provide, rather than surreptitiously pulling strings that far exceed their remit.

One problematic consequence of this type of managerial approach to community formation is its dismissal of extant social and political circumstances that give an organic shape to public life and community interactions. When the managerial imperative attempts to short-circuit these realities, the result can be the superficial appearance of community, but one that has failed to challenge the underlying fractiousness in society. Often, the only way of maintaining this appearance is to introduce further regulatory measures and social controls which silence those elements prone to disagree, but who consequently are stripped of a forum in which to express their disagreement.

The proliferation of controls over the design and use of public space highlight the manner in which the spectacle of community takes precedence over a genuine sense of public interaction. One only has to look at the interactions of the young and the elderly to understand how common it is to come across different sections of society who occupy the same space, but who are mutually suspicious and clearly remain estranged from each other (Holland *et al.* 2007). Public space can be well designed and provide an environment for different members of the public to occupy, but it cannot create a sense of being public; that is something which can only emerge from a genuine sense of debate, argument and interaction.

Unfortunately the latter is usually played down in favour of lauding the benefits of design as a means to mould better citizens and maintain a spectacle of community. This is clear from New Labour's favourite architect Lord Richard Rogers. Taking the sentiment expressed by Jean-Jacques Rousseau in *The Social Contract* that 'houses may make a town, while only citizens can make a city' (Rousseau 1762: 16), Rogers bastardises it by suggesting 'people make cities, but cities make citizens' (ODPM 2000: 7). However, the suggestion that well-designed urban squares can create citizens ends up undermining the often messy but more fulsome business of active citizens working through what they want from city life. Without this process, at the end of the day, divisions are more likely to have been institutionalised rather than resolved. When Rogers adds that 'cities need citizens' (Rogers and Power 2000), it is clear that for some people at least, this deactivated sense of citizenship which is played out in the pavement cafes of orderly public squares is less a cause for concern than of contentment at the reassuring spectacle of community life.

The ubiquitous tier of 'community creators' has become so commonplace because most discussion on community accepts the premise that underlying the problem of community is an excessive individualism, which must be tamed and stitched back into community under the supervision of those in a position of authority. The chapters in this book tell a very different story. We find that it is the trend towards ever greater levels of technical control, community management and regulation of everyday life that is the key problem.

Increasingly, the space that people need to develop relationships with others under their own dynamic and to test out for themselves what works and what doesn't is denied them. When community relations become subsumed within a regulatory framework, with someone in authority constantly pulling the strings, the incentive for spontaneous relations with others diminishes. In such a regulatory scenario, relations lack a genuine sociability, stripped as they are of those informal processes through which people interact of their own free will, and develop confidence and trust in their relations with others. Instead of looking to neighbours and friends as potential allies, there is an increasing tendency nowadays to call on institutions to instigate a framework of risk management that can protect us from what we see as the potentially awkward or dangerous neighbours. With practically every government and local government initiative formatted to facilitate greater levels of intervention, and a proliferating number of state agencies aiming to tame these everyday tensions by engineering community into existence, powerful forces are at work that undercut any sense of individual responsibility and empowerment.

Some, the RSA's Matthew Taylor for example (Taylor 2007), formally recognise the need for citizens to choose for themselves how to act responsibly and wisely. Yet this is just a notional freedom of choice, entwined as it is with the more powerful conviction that government must encourage the right choices. But if communities are not to be allowed the space to choose for themselves what acting responsibly means, then the only question becomes which organisation of officialdom will be the one to ensure the right interpretation of 'responsible' and 'wise'. It seems that in the absence of a broader framework for giving direction to society as a whole, genuine individual choice is off limits given that it is implied that individuals can't be trusted to make the right decision. Real choice has thus been interpreted as a real or implied threat to social stability.

The outlook for recreating a new sense of citizenship is, however, far from bleak. The capacity of individuals to take responsibility for themselves and to make common cause with others – be they neighbours, workmates or even comparative strangers – remains, and often asserts itself even under the most difficult of circumstances. A colleague at University College Hospital in central London once relayed to me his surprise at the hitherto unseen levels of individual initiative and cooperation on display in the immediate aftermath of the 7/7 bombings (one of which was near the hospital). It has been widely recognised that even in the face of appalling circumstances, people have an inspiring capacity spontaneously to organise themselves in a collective fashion to deal with all eventualities. In much more mundane circumstances, whether for social enjoyment, at work, or for practical purposes within neighbourhoods, people organise their interactions free from official guidance on a daily basis.

As Martyn Perks notes, given new technological means at our disposal, in many ways our capacity for interaction with others is potentially far more advanced now than ever before. Yet at the moment we seem to lack a framework that can give such connections a more consistently worthwhile form. Of course the route through which a new sense of public and citizenship might be shaped is not entirely obvious; history suggests these things tend to be worked out as we go along rather than to a blueprint. Yet an obvious precondition is a space that is free of the distorting influences of endless bureaucratic initiatives designed to engage us.

If, as Andrew Calcutt suggests, the emergence of a personalised form of community in the post-war period coincided with the shrinking of political space, then perhaps the question we need to answer now is how we go about creating a new political space within society that serves to free communities from the destructive interventions of officialdom. Ultimately, it is only if we are free to debate and argue over what form community relations take that a genuine sense of citizenship can occur. To achieve this, a discussion on the creation of 'active citizens' needs to be removed from the narrow confines of the official 'engagement' discussion. To achieve this will require asserting our right to take decisions independently, and taking responsibility for our own lives. Conflicts will undoubtedly be part of the process, but only by addressing rather than smoothing over the conflicts will a framework develop in society that gives shape and purpose to public interaction. Only then can we determine, by common agreement, the boundaries of how we wish to relate to others within the community.

There is undoubtedly a very real dimension to the sense that society has become more individuated and atomised, and it is clear today that to some extent we stand estranged from others. But the key lesson is that the attempt to manage a more positive form of social relations back into existence will not work – it can only serve to reinforce the nature of the problem by undermining our capacity to act for ourselves and to decide our own priorities. The re-creation of social solidarity can only emerge in unity with a broader challenge to the current of anxiety that often short-circuits the formation of organic relationships between people. This only makes sense as part of a new political and cultural framework that embraces both the active community and the autonomous individual. Hopefully the chapters in *Future of Community* are an important contribution to a wider political debate about the future of community – and what this says about the individuals that will constitute it, and their relationship to each other, and to society more broadly.

REFERENCES

Cameron, D. (2007) 'Cameron calls for culture change to combat "anarchy in the UK"', *Guardian*, 20 August

Holland, C., Clark, A., Katz, J. and Peace, S. (2007) *Social Interactions in Urban Public Places*, Bristol, Policy Press

ODPM (2000) 'Our towns and cities: the future', White Paper

Rogers, R. and Power, A. (2000) *Cities for a Small Country*, London, Faber and Faber

Rousseau, J.-J. (1762) *The Social Contract* (2004 edition) London, Penguin

Taylor, M. (2007) 'Pro-social behaviour: the future – it's up to us', www.rsa.org.uk/acrobat/pro-social_behaviour.pdf (accessed 11 May 2008)

Contributors

Dr Andrew Calcutt is principal lecturer in journalism at the University of East London, where he leads the master's programme in Journalism and Society. He is a member of the London East Research Institute and editor of its online journal *Rising East* (www.risingeast.org). His first book was *Arrested Development: Pop Culture and the Erosion of Adulthood* (London, Cassell 1998) and he is now working on *The Mediation Nation: Britain's Social Role after Empire and the Cold War.*

Dave Clements is a freelance writer on social policy and related issues, a founding member of the Future Cities Project, and also works as a policy officer in children's social care. His professional background is in local government and he lives and works in East London. He has written widely for publications including *Guardian Unlimited*, *The Architects' Journal*, *spiked* and *Community Care Magazine*, and regularly debates on public platforms.

Neil Davenport is a lecturer in politics and sociology at the JFS Sixth Form Centre in Middlesex. He is the co-author of *The Lecturers Guide to Further Education* (Milton Keynes, Open University Press 2007). He currently researches on how multiculturalism is creating new power relations in society.

Suzy Dean is a freelance journalist and writer. She regularly writes on the subjects of multiculturalism and democracy for publications including *openDemocracy* and *spiked*.

Alastair Donald is an urban designer. His is currently a research student at the Martin Centre for Architectural and Urban Studies at Cambridge University. Alastair is a regular contributor to *Urban Design* and a founder member of ManTownHuman who published the *Manifesto: Towards a New Humanism in Architecture* in 2008.

Martin Earnshaw was a convenor of The Future of Community conference and a founding member of the Future Cities Project. He devised and authored the 'Attitudes to the City' report examining perceptions of crime and anti-social behaviour. Currently, he runs the Future Cities Projects Readers Group, is reviews editor for the Future Cities Project website, and has written for *Culture Wars* and the Battle of Ideas 'Battles in Print' Series.

Elisabetta Gasparoni-Abraham – after working as a teacher for eight years, Elisabetta worked in London researching the urban environment. She has a degree in foreign languages, a masters on German playwright Frank Wedekind, and has worked as a consultant of Italian Language and Literature at the Education Department of the City Council of Milan. Elisabetta is currently studying on the Masters Italian Studies Program in San Francisco State University Department of Foreign Languages and Literatures as well as working as an art and architectural correspondent.

Penny Lewis is the former editor of *Prospect*, the Scottish architecture magazine. She has written about architecture and broader cultural and social issues for the *Herald*, the *Scotsman*, the *Sunday Times*, the *Independent*, *Building Design* and *RIBA Journal*. She is co-author of *In Defence of the Dome* (London, Adam Smith Institute 1998) and author of a monograph on the Scottish architects Gordon Murray and Alan Dunlop Architects. She currently lectures in architectural theory and history at the Scott Sutherland School of Architecture and the Built Environment in Aberdeen.

Martyn Perks is a design consultant. He has written about design, technology and innovation for a number of publications including *spiked*, *Blueprint*, *New Media Age*, and the *Guardian*'s arts&entertainment blog. He has also organised and spoken at events at the Design Council and the Design Museum. In 2007 he convened the Battle for Innovation for the Battle of Ideas festival. See www.martynperks.com.

Karl Sharro is an architect and writer. Before relocating to the UK, he worked on several building projects in downtown Beirut and taught at the Department of Architecture and Design at the American University of Beirut. While there he participated in various research projects on post-war reconstruction and urban renewal. Karl has written for a number of international publications, such as *Springerin* (Austria), *Mark Magazine* (Holland), *Blueprint* (UK) and *NOVO* (Germany). He has spoken on a range of issues around art, architecture and the city.

Dr Stuart Waiton is a sociology lecturer at Abertay Dundee University, a director of the research group Generation Youth Issues, and a regular contributor to the *Times Educational Supplement* in Scotland. He is author of *The Politics of Antisocial Behaviour: Amoral Panics* (London, Routledge 2008).

Austin Williams is the author of *The Enemies of Progress: The Dangers of Sustainability* (Exeter, Societas 2008) and is author and illustrator of *Shortcuts: Essential Guides for Building Designers* (London, RIBA Publishing 2008). He is the founder member of ManTownHuman (www.mantownhuman.org).

Dr Richard Williams is director of the Graduate School of Arts, Culture and Environment at the University of Edinburgh. He is author of *The Anxious City* (London, Routledge 2004), *After Modern Sculpture* (Manchester, Manchester University Press 2000), and *Brazil: Modern Architectures in History* (London, Reaktion Books 2008).

Index